ITCHING FOR IDEAS

Hundreds Of Creative Activities for Classroom Success

by Sylvia Gay, Janet Hoelker,
Kathryn Reithal, and Sharifa Townsend

Incentive Publications, Inc.
Nashville, Tennessee

Cover and illustrations by Cheryl Mendenhall
Edited by Sherri Y. Lewis

ISBN 0-86530-207-3

© Copyright 1991 by Incentive Publications, Inc., Nashville, TN. All rights reserved. No part of this publication may be reproduced, stored in a retrieval system, or transmitted in any form or by any means (electronic, mechanical, photocopying, recording, or otherwise) without prior written permission from Incentive Publications, Inc., with the exception below.

Permission is hereby granted to the purchaser of one copy of ITCHING FOR IDEAS to reproduce, in sufficient quantities for meeting yearly classroom needs.

TABLE OF CONTENTS

Introduction..7

Nature's Nuances
Sun & Clouds..11
Moon & Stars..12
Rain..14
Wind...16
Snow...17
Fish/Ocean..18
Eggs..20
Seeds & Plants...22
Ants...23
Butterflies/Caterpillars..24
Worms..25
Bees..28
Squirrels...30
Owls..32

Getting To Know You
Chef..35
Friends..36
Mail Carrier...38
Homemaker..40
Teacher..42

Going Places
Ice Cream...45
Circus..46
Library...48
Groceries...50
Restaurant...52

Dress 'Em Up
Winter Wear..55
Clothes...56
Fasteners...59
Shoes, Socks, & Feet..62
Hats...65

Holiday Spirits
Bells 69
Elves 72
Ornaments 74
Reindeer 76
Wreaths 78
Scarecrows 80
Pilgrims 82
Indians 84
Turkeys 87

Useful Items
Object Functions 91
Furniture 92
Tools 94
Vehicles 96
Telephone 98

Not-So-Boring Basics
Body Parts 101
Colors 103
Left/Right 106
Shapes 108
Prepositions 111
Letters & Numbers 114

Skills Charts
Nature's Nuances 119
Getting To Know You 120
Going Places 121
Dress 'Em Up 122
Holiday Spirits 123
Useful Items 124
Not-So-Boring Basics 125
Blank Chart 126
Notes 127

INTRODUCTION

ITCHING FOR IDEAS is the comprehensive resource that you have been looking for to help you turn unplanned and/or unexpected blocks of free time into teachable moments.

Quick and easily implemented high-interest activities are presented in a creative and challenging manner to make teacher lesson planning easier and classroom dynamics more exciting.

This collection includes supplementary and enrichment activities in areas ranging from science, social studies, art, and holidays, to basic skills and more.

Thoughtfully divided into helpful sections including: Nature's Nuances, Getting To Know You, Going Places, Dress 'Em Up, Holiday Spirits, Useful Items, and Not-So-Boring Basics, you can tell at a moment's glance which activity best meets your needs at the time. Choose a category from the table of contents, check the skills chart in the back section for skills emphasis, then select an activity from the several in that category that correlates best with your lesson plan! There's even a blank skills chart to categorize your own "instant ideas"!

Let ITCHING FOR IDEAS end your "scratching" for ideas!

NATURE'S NUANCES

SUN & CLOUDS

FLOATING ON A CLOUD

One child sits on a large white pillow (cloud) and is pulled back and forth by other children. He/she tells the class things that he/she "sees" while looking down to earth.
Materials: Large white pillow

SUNGLASSES

Cut or have the children cut glasses' frames out of paper plates. Let them decorate these with macaroni, paint, crayons, etc.
Materials: Paper plates, various materials with which to decorate glasses

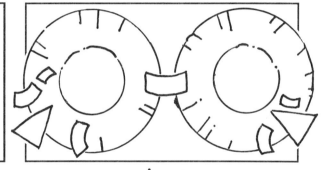

SUN DANCE KID

Make a sun ray hat by attaching paper cones to a strip of paper long enough to fit around the child's face with yarn ties at either end. The "sun" stands inside the circle dancing/rotating on his/her own axis as the other children dance around the sun while singing.

Tune – "Do, re, me, fa, so, la, ti, do. Do, ti, la, so, fa, me, re, do."

The sun is hot. It gives us light.

We do not see the sun at night.

Materials: Paper, yarn, scissors, tape or glue

MOON & STARS

STAR GAZE
Paste stars with different attributes (big, small, yellow, red, missing a point, half a star, etc.) on a chalkboard or on a large black sheet of paper. Make a "telescope" using a paper towel roll. Have the children look through the "telescope" to locate a particular star.
Materials: Stars with different attributes, chalkboard or black paper, paper towel roll decorated as a telescope
Variation: Find the two stars that are the same, different, opposite, etc.

FINDING A STAR
Cut out paper stars. Put vocabulary pictures, letters, or numbers, etc., on each star. Tape stars to the ceiling and turn out the lights. Each child should take a turn shining the flashlight to find a star. Have the child identify what is on the star.
Materials: Flashlight, paper stars, pictures, numbers, letters, scissors, tape, marker

MAN ON THE MOON
Cut out half moons from paper plates. Draw a variety of profiles depicting expressions (happy, sad, surprised, mad, etc.) on paper plate halves. Staple string/yarn to each moon. Make stars with a variety of expressions corresponding to the moon. Have children clip or tape the appropriate stars to the strings hanging from each moon.
Materials: Paper plates, yarn, construction paper, paper clips or clothespins, scissors, tape, stapler
Variation: Write a numeral on each moon and have children clip/tape the appropriate number of stars to each moon.
Variation II: Print a consonant on each moon and have the children attach stars with the picture depicting the corresponding sound.

WALKING ON THE MOON

Have the children take turns wearing "moon boots." (These boots are made from large sponges attached to the feet with strong rubber bands. Plastic snowboots can be used.) Using a thick gymnastic mat, have the children pretend they are walking on the moon. Have them take high and low steps.

Materials: Snowboots, large sponges, strong rubber bands, thick gymnastic mat

STAR PICTURES

Provide illustrations, pictures, or books depicting the different constellations found in the sky. Make a stamp pad using several thicknesses of paper towels. Using a star-shaped sponge, have children sponge-paint along lines of drawn shapes or objects to make their own "constellations." If possible, attach constellations to the ceiling so children can lie on the floor and look at the "sky" and the "stars." Children can also make a telescope using paper towel or toilet paper rolls.

Materials: Paper towels, sponges which have been cut in the shape of stars, large pieces of paper with drawn objects/shapes on them, yellow or white paint, paper towel or toilet paper rolls

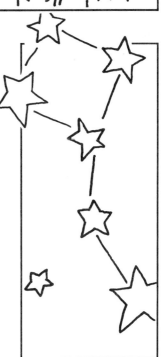

COUNT THE STARS

Cover the inside of shoe box lids with fluorescent paper. Punch a desired quantity of holes in pieces of black construction paper and glue them over the fluorescent paper in each lid. Turn off the lights and have the children count the number of stars they see in each "sky" lid.

Materials: Hole punch, fluorescent paper, black paper, shoe box lids, glue

Variation: Use a black light during the activity.

RAIN

RAINDROPS FALLING ON MY BODY
Cut out the same number of raindrops as children. Give each child a raindrop. Sing the line of the song "Raindrops Keep Falling On My Head." Change the last word to different body parts. Let the children place their raindrop on the specific body part mentioned. Let them suggest body parts.
Materials: Construction paper raindrops

RAIN PUDDLES
Cut out several rain puddles, and tape a path around the room or outside. Put a pair of boots and an umbrella at the end of the path. Let the child run around the puddles to get to the boots, put them on, raise the umbrella, and return by "splashing" in each puddle.
Materials: Large paper, boots, umbrella, tape, scissors

PITTER, PATTER
Discuss with the children how the rain makes a pitter patter noise when it hits the ground. Tell them they must follow what you do to make the pitter patter sound by patting their legs with their hands. Vary the sequence and pattern each time, – fast, slow, loud, soft. After several demonstrations, allow the children to take turns being the leader and tapping out patterns for the others to follow.
Materials: None

RAINDROPS

Using an eyedropper/medicine dropper, let the children drop "raindrops" onto dark paper.

Materials:
Eyedropper/medicine dropper, dark paper, liquid (water, paint, etc.)

BEWARE OF THE PUDDLE

Cut several puddles out of blue paper about the size of a paper plate. Place the puddles in a row a few feet apart. Have the children try to step over the puddles without touching and getting their feet wet. To increase the level of difficulty, have the children try to jump over each puddle. Increase the distance between the puddles with each trial.

Materials: Construction paper, scissors

CLOUDS AND RAIN

Cut out ten clouds. Number them from one to ten. Glue one cloud on the top of ten separate sheets of paper. Laminate, if possible. Have the children draw the corresponding number of raindrops.

Materials: Paper, washable markers, scissors, glue

Variation: Give each child cutout raindrops to match.

WIND

BLOWING LEAVES
Have the children sit at a table. Give each child a paper plate with a pile of tissue paper leaves that have been cut out of fall colors. Tell the children they should pretend to be the wind, and on the count of three, they must try to blow all their leaves off the plate.
Materials: Tissue paper, paper plates

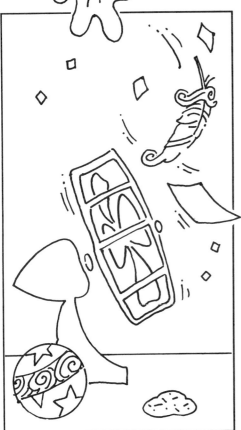

BLOW, WIND, BLOW
Select a variety of light and heavy objects (cotton balls, scarf, tissue, feather, paper, styrofoam, book, rock, ball, pan lid). Have a fan available. As you present each object to the children, ask whether or not they think the wind from the fan will blow the object. Turn on the fan and drop the object in front of the fan. Observe and then discuss what happens.
Materials: Fan, light and heavy objects
Variation: After you complete the above activity using all the objects, present the objects again. This time ask the children if they recall what happened when the object was dropped in front of the wind.
Variation II: Ask the children to pretend they are the objects. Ask them to imitate the movement of the objects in the wind (feather – floats, rock – drops, ball – rolls). "Fan" the children, also.
Caution – adult monitoring of fan is necessary.

WIND
Tune – "I'm A Little Teapot"
I'm the strong wind, and I blow and blow.
I tease the leaves and swirl the snow.
I blow very hard or I blow very soft.
I like to play and blow your hat off!
(Child throws hat off head.)
Materials: Hat

SNOW

MAKE A SNOWBALL

Give each child some white clay. Pretend that it is snow. Have the children practice making a snowball. Then have them make a specific number of snowballs, different sized ones, etc. Have the children stack snowballs to make a fort, snowman, etc.

Materials: White clay

NIGHT SNOW PICTURES

Paste houses on black construction paper. Spread glue on the picture as desired. Have children shake salt or glitter on paper as snow.

Materials: Black construction paper, paper houses, glue, glitter, salt, salt shaker

PAPER BAG SNOWMAN

Have the children stuff three bags (small, medium, and large) with newspaper. Tie each bag. Have the children paint each bag white. Stack the bags on top of each other to form a snowman. Fasten bags to each other with masking tape. Paint or glue facial features on the snowman. Glue on buttons; wrap material around neck as shown.

Materials: Paper bags (small, medium, large), white and black paint, masking tape, string, material strips, buttons, construction paper

FISH/OCEAN

FISH OUTLINE
On a large piece of blue paper, draw outlines of a variety of fish or creatures that live in the ocean. Use distinctive shaped fish – starfish, an octopus, sharks, whales, big/small fish, etc. Have children match construction paper fish/creatures that live in the ocean to the proper outline.
Materials: Paper, precut fish or ocean creatures, markers, crayons

WHAT DID YOU SEE IN THE SEA?
Place a variety of objects in a container which will represent the "ocean" (e.g., pool, large box painted blue, blue blanket, etc.). Tell the children they are going to dive in the ocean and they must remember everything they see. Call on children individually to dive into the sea while the rest of the class sings the song below. The "diver" must return to the group by the last line of the song and tell what he/she saw.

(Tune – "A Sailor Went To Sea")

_____ (child's name) went to sea, sea, sea,

to see what he/she could see, see, see.

But all that _____ (name) could see, see, see,

was __ __ (child names items he/she saw).

Materials: Container that represents the ocean, variety of familiar objects
Variation: Winner can be the child who remembers the most from a static group. The teacher may change items for several trials.
Variation II: Tell the children that there is a treasure hidden among the items and they can find the treasure (candy, raisins, etc.) as they look through the items.

SILLY FISH
Paste construction paper fish on a piece of paper. Let the children add silly features (legs, arms, wings, etc.) to create silly fish.
Materials: Construction paper fish, markers, crayons, etc.

FISH SCALES

Cut three to four large fish with "flexible" scales out of paper. Put a variety of different category pictures on individual scales (toys, animals, fruits, etc.). The children should sort the pictures by "things that go together" and then put all those scales on the same fish.

Materials: Paper pictures or drawings depicting different categories

Variation: Use pictures of objects on scales; match scales to correct beginning sound of letter drawn on a fish.

EXPERIMENTAL FISH

Collect various items that will sink and float. Using waterproof markers, draw a fish on each item. Fill a large bin or bowl with water to represent a pond. Have children place "fish" in the water to determine if they will sink or float.

Materials: Items that sink (metal, rocks, etc.), items that float (styrofoam, jar lid, hard plastic, small balloon, etc.), waterproof markers, bin or bowl, water

SEAHORSE VS. "LAND" HORSE

Describe seahorses to the children. Talk about where they live, what they eat, how they move. Compare and contrast them to a "land" horse. Tape finger puppets of each for the children to wear during the discussion.

Materials: Paper, tape, markers, scissors

EGGS

COLORED EGGS

Make birds' nests by covering plastic tubs with different colored construction paper. Have children sort different colored plastic eggs into same color nests.

Materials: Colored plastic eggs, plastic tubs, construction paper, glue

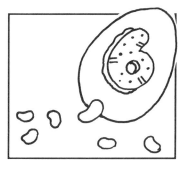

NUMBER EGGS

Write a numeral inside each plastic egg. The children put a quantity of jelly beans in chosen egg to match the printed numeral.

Materials: Plastic eggs, markers, jelly beans

WHAT'S IN THE EGG?

In different colored plastic eggs, put a picture of a different animal which is hatched from an egg (turtle, duck, snake, fish, etc.). Bury the eggs in sand, place them in a nest, or hide them around the room. Give the children a description of the animal they are to locate, e.g., "This animal hatches from an egg. He has no feathers. He crawls because he has no legs."

Have one child select an egg and explain why it is or is not the correct animal. (The children should begin to remember that a certain colored egg contains a particular animal.)

Materials: Plastic eggs, egg-hatched animal pictures, sand/nest

Variation: All the eggs can be the same color.

EGG CARTON/ EGGSHELLS

Draw an outline of an egg on a piece of construction paper. Have the children break up styrofoam egg cartons and glue the pieces onto the egg.

Materials: Styrofoam egg cartons, paper, glue, marker

EGGHEAD PUZZLE

Cut eggs from construction paper. Draw a variety of eyes on the top of each egg and a variety of mouths on the bottom of each one. Cut a jagged line across the center of each egg to form individual egg puzzles. Mix all the pieces and have the children put the puzzles together.

Materials: Construction paper, scissors, markers

Variation: Cut the same jagged line across all the eggs so the parts can be interchanged to make "silly" faces.

EGG YOLK

Cut out fried egg whites approximately 6 to 8 inches in diameter. Cut out an equal number of yellow yolks and write numerals on the yolks. In the center of each egg white, glue a different quantity of chicks. (Stickers work nicely.) The child should count chicks on the egg whites and cover them with the appropriately numbered yolks.

Materials: White and yellow construction paper, chick stickers, scissors, glue

21

SEEDS & PLANTS

GARDEN OF CHILDREN
Trim the edges of paper plates to form petals. Cut out the center of the plate for the child's face. Attach yarn pieces to either side of the plate to tie on the child's head. You may want to let the children decorate their flowers with crayons, markers, etc. The children should act out a flower growing. Begin by squatting down with arms covering head. As the poem continues, children grow (stand up) unfolding their leaves (arms).

> Some little seeds waiting to grow,
> Water and sun, and up they go!
> Up to the sky with pretty tops,
> Then out their leaves and petals pop!

Materials: Paper plates, yarn, crayons, markers, scissors
Variation: Have one child be the gardener and tap each child on the head when it is time to grow.

WATCH IT GROW
Let children paint a small gelatin box brown/black to represent dirt. Make a small slit in the bottom of the box in which a tongue depressor will fit. Draw a small green plant (stem and leaves) and attach it to the top of the tongue depressor. Insert the stick through the slit in the box. Pull the stick to hide the plant. Have the children drop a seed (bean or paper) into the box. This is the first step in the growing sequence. Have a child gradually push the plant up as the class discusses how the plant grows and becomes bigger and bigger.

Materials: Empty gelatin boxes, tongue depressors, paper, tape, paint, scissors

CATEGORY FLOWERS
Cut out large construction paper petals and a circle for the flower's center. Put pictures of category components accompanied by a complementary word printed on each petal. Let children sort the petals and match to the appropriate centers forming a flower. (This may be a group activity or an individual activity to take home.)

Materials: Construction paper, category pictures
Variation: Various uses of a common object may be incorporated by matching the center of the objects with the petals depicting various actions.
Variation II: Illustrate various actions carried out with a common object on each petal. The flower center would be the common object, e.g.,
center – string; petals – tying a box, flying a kite, tying a shoe; etc.

ANTS

THE PICNIC ANT

Tell the children that they will have to look closely and remember what is put into the picnic basket. Depending on each child's memory skill, put two to four items in the basket. Let the class recite this chant:

> We opened the basket
> And what did we see?
> A _____ , _____ , _____ ,
> And a big old ant looking at me.

Materials: Picnic basket or box with a lid, items to put in basket (e.g., spoons, forks, cups, food items, toys, etc.), toy ant

ANTEATER

Provide each child with a paper plate that has four ant hills drawn on each. Write a number on each ant hill. Give each child a bag of raisins and have him/her place the appropriate quantity of ants on each hill. Then tell the children they are anteaters, and have them put their hands behind their backs. Have a race to see who can eat all their ants.

Materials: Raisins, paper plates, markers

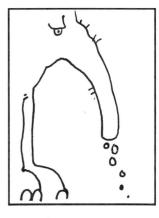

ANTS ON THE HILL

Glue a small margarine container or a strong paper bowl (open side facing down) to a piece of paper (this is the hill). Cut out an entrance to the hill. Dip the end of a cotton swab in black paint. Have the children make ants in, on, and over the hill using the cotton swab. Teach the children the following poem:

> The ants are in,
> The ants are out,
> The ants are crawling all about!

Materials: Margarine container or strong paper bowl (one for each child), construction paper, cotton swabs, glue, black paint

BUTTERFLIES/ CATERPILLARS

FUZZY CATERPILLAR
Use a large plastic play tunnel as a cocoon. Children crawl in one end and come "flying" out the other while the class says this poem:

In went the fuzzy caterpillar,
In a cocoon to rest.
Out came a butterfly,
Looking his/her very best.

Materials: Plastic play tunnel

MATCHING WINGS
Draw an equal number of dots on separated sides of butterfly wings. Each child should find two wings with the same amount of dots to form a butterfly.
Materials: Construction paper, marker
Variation: Put the numeral on one side of the wings and the corresponding number of dots on the other side.

BUTTERFLY WINGS
Cut out pairs of large paper wings for butterflies. Tape the wings to newspaper on the floor. Let the children shake a brush over the wings to splatter paint. Use several different colors. Allow the paint to dry, then hang the butterflies.
Materials: Paper, newspaper, paint, tape, scissors, paintbrush

WORMS

WORM TRAILS

Fit a piece of construction paper into the bottom of a cake pan. Dip two or three marbles in mud (or paint) the consistency of pudding. Tip the pan back and forth and see the "worm trails" appear. After the mud (paint) dries, have the children trace the paths with their fingers.

Materials: Square or circular cake pan, marbles, paint, construction paper

Variation: Dip string in mud (or paint) and drag it across paper to make worm trails.

ROLL A WORM

For a snack, make butter cookie dough. Drop in red and green food coloring to turn the dough brown. Have the children roll the dough into "worms." Bake the worms and EAT!

Materials: Butter cookie dough, food coloring

THE WORM'S ON ME

Cut out fingers of old gloves. Have the children stuff these with tissue paper. The teacher should stitch or staple the ends. Let the children draw facial features on the worm or use buttons and other odds and ends to glue or sew on the worm. Then give each other instructions such as:

Put the worm on your knee.

First put the worm on your shoulder, then put it on your nose.

Materials: Old gloves, tissue paper, markers, needle and thread or stapler

Variation: Use tube socks or gummy worms

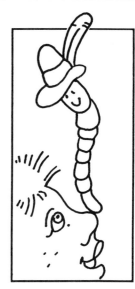

WORMS IN THE APPLE
Finger-paint a very large apple shape (3' x 3'). Cut a hole near the bottom of the apple for the worms (children) to crawl through. Count the worms as they come out of the apple.
Materials: Red finger paint, large piece of paper, scissors

WORM HOLES
Cut out different sized worms – fat to skinny. On a large piece of construction paper, make various sized slits to represent worm holes. Vary the sizes of the holes to match the worms. Laminate if possible. Children should try and visually decide which worm fits in which hole. Then let them put the worms in the holes to check their decisions.
Materials: Construction paper with holes, paper worms, scissors
Variation: Put numbers on the holes and corresponding dots on the worms. Match.

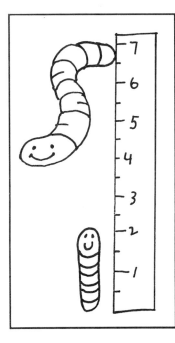

HOW MANY INCHES?
Cut out a number of worms of varying lengths. Have children measure each worm using a ruler or tape measure. Discuss longest, shortest, and how much longer one worm is than another. Put worms in sequential order – longest to shortest.
Materials: Construction paper or yarn worms, tape measure or ruler
Variation: Give each child a ball of clay to roll on the table back and forth into a worm. Have children use a ruler to measure their worms. Let them identify which one is the longest and shortest. Also, let them explore and discover how worms can move, turn, or change position.

THE WORMS CRAWL IN, THE WORMS CRAWL OUT

Have the children fill a barrel/tunnel with "dirt" (styrofoam pieces, torn newspaper, brown construction paper, etc.). After the barrel/tunnel is full, let each child pretend to be a worm and crawl into the "dirt," "eat" some, and crawl out the other side.
Materials: Barrel/tunnel, torn pieces of paper or styrofoam

WIGGLE WORM

Have two children hold each end of a rope and wiggle it on the floor. Have the other children jump over the rope (worm) without stepping on the worm and squashing it.
Materials: Rope

NYLON WORMS

Cut old nylons into 15 inch pieces. Tie one end of each piece. Have students fill pieces with old newspaper or rags. Sew on eyes (material or paper).
Materials: Nylon pieces, old newspaper or material

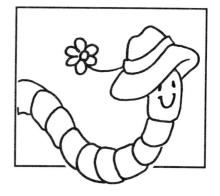

BEES

HONEY HIVES
Have the children spread honey on rice cakes. Place rolled oat cereal on top to look like honeycomb. Place raisins in each piece of cereal to represent bees.
Materials: Honey, rice cakes, raisins, rolled oat cereal

BUZZING AROUND
Talk about how bees get nectar from flowers to make honey. Make construction paper flowers of different colors to hang around the room. Let each child pretend to be the "Queen Bee" and wear a plastic headband with two pipe cleaners with cotton balls attached to each end for an antenna. Direct "Queen Bee" to fly to a specified flower, and bring the detachable center representing the nectar back to the hive.
Materials: Different colors of construction paper flowers with detachable centers, headband, two pipe cleaners, cotton balls
Variation: Make different sized flowers to incorporate two component commands (i.e., get the nectar from the big, red flower).

BEES IN THE HIVE
Divide a large piece of paper (12" x 16") into eight squares. In each square, draw a hive. Put a number on each hive. Make an ink pad by pouring yellow paint on several thicknesses of paper towels or on a sponge. Let the children dip a thumb in the paint and make thumbprint bees to correspond to the number on each hive.

A BEE IN MY BONNET

Make paper plate bonnets with flowers sticking up. Paste a bee on each flower.

Materials: Paper plates, string/ribbon/yarn, construction paper flowers, pipe cleaners for stems, cutout bees

BEE HIVE

Have the children cut out a 7" bee hive. Staple it on a piece of 11½" x 18" paper making sure the center of the hive is elevated approximately 1 inch from the paper for a three-dimensional effect. Cut out, paste, and count bees around, inside, and outside the bee hive.

Materials: Construction paper, scissors, paste, stapler, cutout bees

Variation: Make fingerprint bees by painting fingers yellow and placing on paper. After fingerprint dries, add stripes, wings, head, and stinger with a black pen.

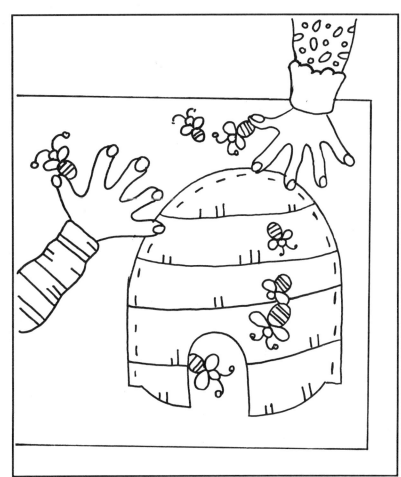

ENVELOPE BEES

Cut the flap off an envelope. Put fingertips in one corner, and put the thumb in the opposite corner. Bring fingertips to thumb with fingertips on top. This will be for the puppet. Cut out wings for the sides, draw black lines on back, and attach antennae.

Materials: Envelope, construction paper for wings and antennae, marker or crayon, colored markers for colorful bees

SQUIRRELS

SQUIRREL BY THE TREE
Squirrel by the tree!
Squirrel by the tree!
What are you doing?
Let us see!
Let one child pretend to be a squirrel and act out anything a squirrel would do: gather acorns/nuts, sit up, climb a tree, etc.
Materials: None

STORING UP FOR WINTER
Collect various sizes of paper tubes. Cover them with brown construction paper and glue paper leaves to the tops. These will be the trees. Have the children pretend to be squirrels saving nuts for the winter. Use real nuts or wooden beads. See how many nuts they can fit in the different sized "trees."
Materials: Paper tubes (from paper towels, toilet tissue, wrapping paper, etc.), green and brown construction paper, nuts or wooden beads

WHOSE TAIL?
Have several felt board animals (squirrel, mouse, bird, pig, etc.) scattered on a felt board. Place their detached tails along the bottom of the board. Ask the children to make silly matches or to make correct matches.
Materials: Cutout felt board animals with detached tails

SQUIRREL'S TAIL

Cut out a variety of squirrels and tails. Have each child match tails to squirrels on the basis of color, numbers/sets, sounds/pictures, sizes, etc.

Materials: Cutout squirrels and tails

Variation: Cut out different colored squirrels and nuts. Have children match same colored nuts and squirrels.

Variation II: Have children match nuts and squirrels based on letters, numerals, etc.

BUSHY TAILS

Cut out large tail shapes. Let the children practice cutting skills by snipping around the tail. When the children finish, let them wear the tails and pretend to be squirrels.

Materials: Brown paper, scissors

THE SQUIRREL AND THE TELEPHONE POLES

Present on a board, floor, or paper, a pattern of telephone poles with connecting wires for a squirrel to run up, across, and down. One of the children can pretend to be the squirrel using a toy squirrel, paper squirrel, or a pencil. At the end of the pattern, the squirrel should find a peanut if he/she completes the pattern. (Emphasize left to right, top to bottom progression, and continual flow.)

Materials: Toy or paper squirrel, peanuts

OWLS

BAGGY OWLS
Cut an owl shape out of tagboard for each student. Cut plastic bags (if possible white or colorful bags) into small petal shapes to use as the breast feathers. Cut wings from brown paper bags. Cut eyes, beak, and feet from meat trays. Let the children assemble.
Materials: Tagboard, plastic bags, meat trays, brown bags, scissors, glue

WHOOO'S HIDING?
Cut several owls out of fluorescent paper. Hide them around the room so a part of each owl is showing. Turn out the lights. Let the children try to find the owls using flashlights.
Materials: Fluorescent paper owls, flashlight, scissors, tape

OWL IN THE TREE
Cut out eight to ten trees giving each tree one to ten branches. Cut out eight to ten owls, and write a numeral (any one from one through ten) on each owl's stomach. Mount the trees on a large board. Attach small magnets to the owls and to the center of the trees. The child should match the correct numbered owl to the tree with the corresponding number of branches.
Materials: Construction paper, scissors, magnets, markers

GETTING TO KNOW YOU

CHEF

BLOCK SOUP

Use different colored blocks to represent ingredients. Make a "recipe" incorporating numbers and colors.

> For example: 2 green blocks
> 1 red block
> 4 yellow blocks

The child should put the designated quantities of blocks in a pan and stir it with a spoon to prepare the recipe.

Materials: Pans, spoons, blocks, recipe cards

COLOR CHEFS

Give each child a different colored chef's hat to cut out, attach to a band, and wear. Spread food picture cards out on a table and have the children find the foods which correspond to the colored chef's hat. After all the foods have been retrieved, the children should take turns naming the items they found, e.g., brown chef – "I made a chocolate cake."

Materials: Construction paper, scissors, glue, picture cards of food

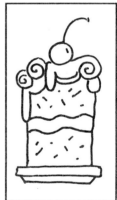

SORTING CHEF

Make three to five large chef figures from cardboard or poster board. Decorate each chef's hat with pictures representing various food groups (vegetables, meat, fruits, dairy, etc.). Make or collect pictures from magazines representing the food groups. Let children sort and place the pictures on the corresponding chef's hat.

Materials: Chef's figure, pictures of components of various food groups

Variation: Choose children to represent the food groups. Make hats for chosen children to wear. Let classmates give pictures to these "real" chefs.

FRIENDS

WHO CAME TO SCHOOL?
Cut out various vehicles, a school building, and a home, and mount them on a bulletin board. Cut slits in vehicles appropriate to hold photographs. Put each student's picture in the vehicle. As student's name is called, he/she locates his/her picture and "drives" to school. Absent students may be identified and taken "home."
Materials: Bulletin board, various vehicles, school, house, student pictures

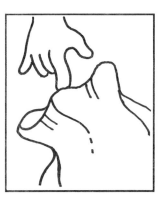

FIND A FRIEND
Put objects that can be shared in a bag. Let one child reach in and pull out an object. He/she should then select a friend to share it. Children should carry out the activity. Then let another child select an object.
Materials: Object to be shared or played with (ball, toy car, wind-up toy, etc.)

HAND MIRROR
Let children pass a hand mirror to each other as the music plays. When the music stops, the child with the mirror in his/her hand holds it out. The teacher asks, "Who has the mirror?" All the children answer with the appropriate name.
Materials: Mirror, music

FRIENDS IN A CIRCLE

Draw a circle on the floor just barely big enough for all the children. If necessary, the circle can be outlined with tape or blocks. To introduce the children to each other, the teacher can say the following verse:

(Name A) is standing in the circle and (he/she) needs a friend.

(Name A) tell (Name B) to, "Come on in."

Each child remains in the circle until all the children have been called. Together the children say:

We're in the circle because we're friends.

We told a friend to, "Come on in."

After several sessions, the children say their own verse:

I'm in the circle and I need a friend.

Hey, (name), come on in.

Materials: Tape or blocks, water soluble markers

Variation: Different shapes and outlines may be substituted for the circle.

LITTLE BOY GREEN

Make pilgrim-type collars in a variety of colors for each child to wear. Call upon each child wearing a certain collar by saying the following rhyme and having him/her act it out:

Little boy/girl blue, tie your shoe.

Little boy/girl yellow is a very sad fellow.

Little boy/girl brown acts like a clown.

Little boy/girl red is going to bed.

Little boy/girl green does not like beans.

Materials: Construction paper, yarn, scissors

PAIR THEM OUT

Use pairs of items (two socks, two gloves, etc.). Separate and give one of each to every child. As each child stands up, he/she asks, "Who has the (other matching item)?" The children look around and answer with, "(Name) has the (item)."

Materials: Pairs of items

Variation: Incorporate association pairs such as toothpaste – toothbrush, sock – shoe, pencil – paper, etc.

MAIL CARRIER

SORT THE MAIL
Compile a variety of different-sized envelopes (letter, legal, thank-you notes, greeting cards, as well as different-sized manila envelopes). The child who is the mail carrier sorts all the envelopes by putting the same-sized envelopes together.
Materials: Various-sized envelopes

OPEN THE MAIL
Put a picture inside an envelope. Glue stamps on the envelopes and write children's names on them. Designate one child as the mail carrier and have him/her deliver the letters. Have each child open an envelope and describe the picture inside.
Materials: Envelopes, pictures on cards

A LETTER FOR MY FRIEND
Draw a rectangle on a piece of paper. Have the children cut out the rectangle as an envelope. To make a stamp, the children should glue on a sticker, a small piece of paper, or draw a stamp on the envelope. Then the teacher prints the names of all the children on labels. Let the children select a name and glue the label on their envelope. During group time, each child should hand out a "letter" to his/her friend. (The teacher should be sure all the students get a letter.)
Materials: Paper, glue, scissors, stickers, crayons, labels
Variation: The children print their friend's name on the envelope.

THE MAIL CARRIER KNOCKS

Set up a divider as a house. Let one child sit behind the divider. Choose another child as the mail carrier to come knocking. The mail carrier knocks a designated number of times and asks, "How many times did I knock?" The child behind the divider answers with the number of knocks he/she heard.

Material: Divider

Variation: Child behind the divider repeats the knocking pattern.

DELIVERY!

Let children pretend to be houses by wearing a necklace with a numeral on it. Choose one child to be the mail carrier. Give him/her cards/letters with numerals on them. The child should deliver the cards to the correct house by matching the numbers.

Materials: Necklaces with numerals, cards/letters with numerals

MISSING MAIL

Have the children sit in a circle. One child is chosen to be the mail carrier, and he/she walks around the circle. The mail carrier has a bag with four or five different colored letters in it. He/she drops his/her bag in front of one of the children and walks away. The child nearest the bag quickly takes out one of the colored letters and hides it behind him/her. The mail carrier comes back to find his/her bag and must look inside and name the color of the letter that is missing.

Materials: Different colored letters, bag

Variation: Pictures can be placed on envelopes.

HOMEMAKER

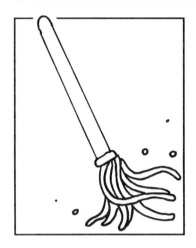

BIG MOPS/ LITTLE MOPS
Make mops by using various lengths of paper towel rolls as the handles. To make the mop head, have the children snip strips around a 3 to 4 inch wide piece of paper. Attach this to the end of the mop handle (paper towel roll). Have the children put the mops in order from shortest to longest, or longest to shortest. Discuss long, longer, longest and short, shorter, shortest.
Materials: Empty paper towel rolls, paper, scissors, tape or glue

STACKING THE CABINETS
Cut various cabinet doors out of brown paper. Mount them on another piece of paper. Cut out and mount pictures of food items, kitchen utensils, etc. On each door, draw a matching picture of one of the kitchen or food items. Have children "put away" the items in the appropriate cabinet.
Materials: Brown construction paper, scissors, glue, small pictures of kitchen and food items
Variation: Put a number on each door. Have children put the designated number of items in each cabinet.

ITEMS NECESSARY TO COMPLETE A TASK
Discuss all the different chores we need to do to keep our houses clean (sweep floor, wash dishes, wash windows, dust furniture, etc.). Collect and display the various utensils/items one needs to complete the tasks. Ask each child what item he/she would need to do a specific chore. Then let him/her act it out, talking about each of the steps.
Materials: Household items

SCRUBBING THE FLOOR

Give each child a pail of water and a sponge. "Scrubbing" in this activity actually entails having the children scrub in various shapes (in a circle, in a square, etc.). Have the children sing as they scrub.

Tune – "Row, Row, Row Your Boat"
Scrub, scrub, scrub the floor.
Scrub it in a _____ (circle, square, etc.).
Scrub, scrub, scrub the floor.
Scrub it in a _____ (circle, etc.).

Materials: Pails, sponges, water
Variation: The children may scrub numerals or letters then let other classmates guess what they made.

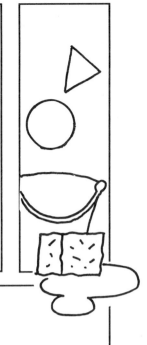

I'M A HOUSEKEEPER

Tune – "London Bridge"
I'm a housekeeper and I mop the floor,
Mop the floor, mop the floor.
I'm a housekeeper and I mop the floor.
Because the floor is dirty.

Other verses: sweep the floor, wash the window, dry the dishes, fold the clothes.
Let the children suggest other things a housekeeper might do. Also, let them brainstorm about why the housekeeper does the chores (last line in song). Act out chores in each verse.

Materials: None

CLEANING UP THE HOUSE

Divide the classroom into pretend rooms of a house. Call upon one child to be the housekeeper and tell him/her to clean up the house. The child should go to the appropriate room and "clean." Sing the following song while the child cleans:

Tune – "Paw Paw Patch"
Picking up clothes and putting them in the basket.
Picking up clothes and putting them in the basket.
Picking up clothes and putting them in the basket.
Gathering the laundry.

Washing the dishes and putting them in the cabinet...
Cleaning up the kitchen.

Fluffing up the pillows and making the bed...
Cleaning up the bedroom.

Running the water and cleaning out the tub...
Cleaning up the bathroom.

Materials: Various household items

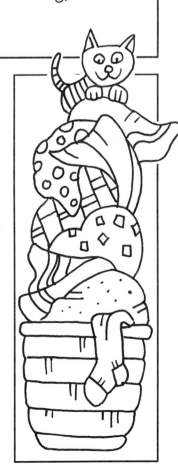

TEACHER

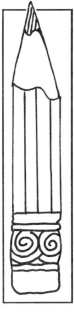

ON THE FIRST DAY OF SCHOOL
Tune – "On the First Day Of Christmas"
On the first day of school, my teacher said to me,
"Put a pencil and some paper on my desk."
On the second day of school, my teacher said to me,
"Put a ruler and a book on my desk."
On the third day of school, my teacher said to me,
"Put an eraser and some chalk on my desk."
On the fourth day of school, my teacher said to me,
"Put an apple and a lunch box on my desk."
On the fifth day of school, my teacher said to me,
"You are good; you may come sit at my desk."
Materials: Desk, pencil, paper, ruler, book, eraser, chalk, apple, lunch box

THE TEACHER'S BAG
Mix teacher and carpenter work items in a box. Let one child pretend to be a teacher and have a teacher's bag. Another child should pretend to be the carpenter with a tool box or tool belt. Let the other children pull items from the box and give them to the correct person.
Materials: Toolbox; teacher's tote bag; various items such as a book, writing paper, ruler, glue, scissors, saw, hammer, screwdriver, etc.

HOW MANY STUDENTS?
Collect a number of small boxes with lids. On each box, write a numeral. These are the classrooms. Cut out several "paper" children. Have the students place the designated number of children in each classroom.
Materials: Small boxes, cutout paper children, scissors

GOING PLACES

ICE CREAM

DIRTY FACES
Provide each child with a laminated face of a boy or girl, a bowl of shaving cream, and a damp cloth. Let the children decide what type of ice cream they want "their friend" to eat, and then give them a couple of drops of the necessary food coloring to stir in the shaving cream (red – strawberry). Then have the children pretend that "their friend" ate the ice cream but was messy and got it all over their face (children smear all over the laminated face). Let them show their dirty faces to each other, then let them use their damp cloths to wipe them clean.
Materials: Laminated boy and girl face drawings, white shaving cream, food coloring, damp cloth towels, small bowls, spoons

NUTTY ICE CREAM
Cut out several scoops of ice cream on which children glue various materials: eggshells, nutshells, sand, rice, fabric, seashells, etc. Assemble three or four scoop cones.
Materials: Various materials, cutout scoops of ice cream, scissors, glue

ANIMAL'S ICE CREAM
Let children choose an animal picture which they show to the other children as they recite the following verse:

You like ice cream, yes you do.
I'm a (giraffe) and I like ice cream, too.
You like chocolate, I can see.
But (grass) ice cream is the kind for me!

Materials: Pictures or facsimiles of animals

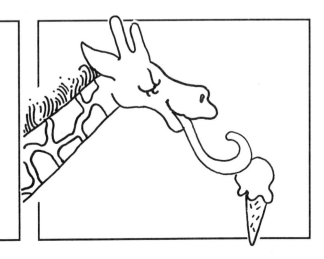

CIRCUS

CIRCUS BANNERS

Let the children trace and cut out triangular banners and decorate them with pictures of animals or scraps of paper. Attach to a stick made from rolled paper. Have a parade with music. Emphasize ordinal positions of animal banners.

Materials: Construction paper, animal pictures, scraps of paper, scissors, glue

FUNNY FACES

Have a child stand behind a large clown body poster facing a mirror. The teacher should stand next to the mirror and have the child try to imitate his/her funny faces.

Materials: Large clown body poster (no head), mirror
Variation: The children try to make the teacher laugh.

CLOWN HAT GROUPS

Make cone shape clown hats out of construction paper. Give each child a different color or category of items to look for in magazines. Have the children cut out and glue the pictures on their clown hats. Play games with hats for categorizing (animal clowns, stand up; fruit clowns, clap your hands; etc.).

Materials: Construction paper, magazine pictures, glue, scissors

FEEDING THE ELEPHANTS

Make a big and little elephant face. Also, make big and little peanuts. Have the children match big peanuts with big elephants and little peanuts with little elephants.

Materials: Construction paper elephants and peanuts

Variation: Count the peanuts.

Variation II: Follow directions (feed two little peanuts to the big elephant).

Variation III: Focus on long and short trunks.

CIRCUS PARADE

Cut out doubles of various circus characters. Line these up in a specific order. Have the children use the other pair and match the order.

Materials: Two sets of cutout circus characters

Variation: Use the parade as a visual memory activity, taking away or adding one character after a child reviews the lineup. The child states which character was removed or added.

CLOWN FACES

Color ten clown faces and hats with slight differences on each one. Mount the clown faces on oaktag, cut out, and prepare back for felt board. The children can describe differences, similarities, or categorize.

Materials: Cutout clown faces, felt, oaktag or poster board, felt board

LIBRARY

PUT THE BOOKS AWAY

Collect a variety of books that deals with one subject/category only (books about animals, food, transportation, etc.). Use large boxes to represent the library shelves. Paste a picture of one category on each shelf. Let the children put the books away by matching the subject of the book to the corresponding category and placing it in the correct box, e.g., a book about a horse should go in the animal box.

Materials: Books, large boxes, magazines, markers, paste

Variation: Instead of using library books, make books. Do this by stapling several pieces of paper together and drawing or gluing on pictures of animals, fruits, toys, etc. Add words if desired.

BIG BOOK/LITTLE BOOK

Use a small child-size shelf, or make one out of a large box or crate. Collect a number of books of varying sizes – big to little. The children should put the books in order on the shelf by arranging the books from the biggest to the smallest.

Materials: Books, shelf, large box

BOOKWORM

Make a bookworm puppet from a sock. Have the bookworm talk to the children and direct them to retrieve familiar books according to the clues the bookworm provides, e.g., "Bring me the book about the caterpillar that eats a lot of food." (Name of book.)

Materials: Long white knee socks, familiar books, table to display books

BOOKS OF A DIFFERENT COLOR

Make covers for books with solid colored construction paper. Make shelves from large cardboard boxes. Paint the shelves to match the book covers. Let the children play librarian and "shelve" (sort) the books by color.

Materials: Construction paper, large cardboard boxes, paint, tape

RIDDLE BOOKS

Make books from cereal boxes by cutting one side open along three edges. Glue on construction paper to cover the flap. On the front of the flap, make a riddle book cover by placing two or three picture clues on it indicating what the book is about. For example, put a patch of yellow and a monkey. When you open the cover, there will be a banana (object or picture). Other ideas can include:

Cover	Inside
Long nose, peanuts, gray	Elephant
Hose, fire truck, ladder	Fireman
Seeds, dirt, leaves	Plant

Materials: Cereal boxes, construction paper, glue, tape, objects or pictures, picture clues

LIBRARY CARD

Let the children draw and cut out medium-sized rectangles to make library cards. Each child should print his/her name on his/her card. Put all the books in one area and designate this as the library. Let the children select one to five books, and the child who is chosen as the librarian punches holes in each card according to the quantity of books "checked out" by each child.

Materials: Paper, books, scissors, markers or crayons, hole punch

GROCERIES

STACK IT UP
Talk about how high the food is sometimes stacked at grocery stores. Let the children stack toilet paper rolls, empty boxes of cereal, cans, etc. Challenge the children to see how high they can stack the items.
Materials: Toilet paper rolls, stored items that are stackable

TO THE GROCERY STORE WE'LL GO
    Tune – "Farmer In The Dell"
    To the grocery store I'll go,
    The grocery store I'll go.
    I'll buy some _____ and _____ and _____ ,
    To the grocery store I'll go.
Put various items on a flannel board or stack them on a table. The child should pick up items as he/she sings.
Materials: Various grocery items

LABEL THE CAN
Talk about how we know what is in the food we buy by looking at the labels. Give each student a can with the label torn off. Tell him/her to shake it and guess what is inside. Let him/her create a label for his/her can. Have one or two for snacks, and discuss what was inside.
Materials: Cans without labels, paper, crayons, tape

WHERE'S THE MEAT?

Place food department pictures all over a large piece of paper and glue them on. Draw an entrance door at the bottom of the paper with separate aisle mazes leading from the door to each of the food departments. Have a child utilize a toy person to follow the appropriate maze to get to the correct food department to purchase an item.

Materials: A large piece of chart paper or poster board, pictures of food, toy person, glue

COUPONS

Make up a "newspaper" with one to five cents off "coupons" which the children can cut out. The children should deduct the value of a coupon from what they buy at the play store.

Materials: Newspaper coupons, various store items, scissors

Variation: Cutout real newspaper coupons.

GROCERY CART RACES

Use two child-size plastic grocery carts. Have the children push carts from point A to point B. At point B, the children should pick up and put a grocery item (can, box, bag, etc.) into their cart and race back to point A.

Materials: Plastic grocery carts, grocery store items

RESTAURANT

MENU MATCH
Pocket file folders can serve as menus with small food pictures placed inside the pockets. The child who is the customer chooses food from the menu by giving food item pictures he/she wishes to order. The waitress matches the customer's selections with real/pretend foods or matching pictures and puts them on the plate. Then the waitress serves them to the customer.

Materials: Apron, plates, chairs, table, pocket file folders, food pictures – either in pairs or facsimiles of food to match pictures, real/pretend foods

PIZZA PLACE
Make or buy cardboard pizza plates – one for each child. Out of construction paper, fabric remnants, wallpaper, etc., make various garnishes (cheese, pepperoni, green peppers, mushrooms, etc.). Designate one student as the pizza maker while others "order" what they want on their pizzas.

Materials: Cardboard pizza plates, construction paper, fabric remnants, textured materials

MAIN MENU
Collect various pictures of different types of food – fruit, meat, ice cream, drinks, etc. Fold a large piece of construction paper in half for a menu. Inside, divide the halves into sections. Have the children sort and paste pictures into proper sections. On the front, let them decorate with their restaurant names.

Materials: Pictures of various types of food, construction paper

DRESS 'EM UP

WINTER WEAR

THERE'S A BOOT ON MY HEAD

Use boots and mittens. Sing the following chorus, and manipulate the boots and mittens according to the song.

Tune – "There's A Hole In My Bucket"

Adult: There's a boot on my head, my head, my head.
There's a boot on my head, my head, a boot.
Children: No, no, on your foot.
All: There's a boot on my foot, my foot, my foot.
There's a boot on my foot, my foot, a boot.

Continue the song and substitute "mitten." Change body parts, putting the boot or mitten on your arm, leg, etc.

Materials: Boots, mittens

"FEELY" MITTENS

Cut out several pairs of mittens made of various materials (burlap, felt, nylon, cardboard, cardboard covered with rice, etc.). Blindfold a child and hand the child one mitten. The child should identify the appropriate pair by feeling the others.

Materials: Mittens of various materials, scissors

HOW MANY DO WE NEED?

Have a supply of mittens and boots, or cut some from construction paper. The number of boots or mittens should be less than the number of children in the group. Have one child hand out boots and mittens to each child until the supply runs out. Some will have only boots and others only mittens. Then ask questions:

Do we have more children than boots? Mittens?
How do you know?
How many more boots and mittens do we need so that everyone has both?
Do we need more mittens or more boots?
How can we get more?
Where?

Continue with questions, and encourage the children to ask questions.

Materials: Boots, mittens, construction paper, scissors

CLOTHES

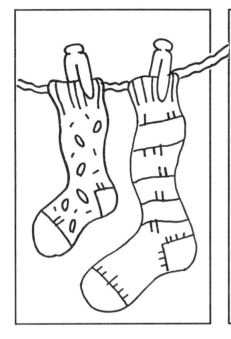

HANG IT UP
Pretend to wash a variety of clothing items in a large wash bin. Hang a clothesline across the room at the children's height. A selected child should pull a clothing item out of the wash bin, name it, and hang it on the clothesline.
Materials: Clothing items, clothespins, wash bin, clothesline
Variation: Cut out a variety of colored pairs of socks, and mix them up in the laundry basket. Let children find a pair and hang them on the clothesline.
Variation II: Match numerals and quantities, associated pairs, upper/lower case letters, patterns.
Variation III: Find two socks that are different.

I'M A MESS!
The teacher should come into the classroom wearing an inside-out blouse or shirt with one short sleeve, one long sleeve, half a collar, the buttons improperly buttoned, etc. Let the children point out the things that are wrong.
Material: Old blouse or shirt
Variation: Other clothing items

CLOTHES HAMPER
In a clothes hamper, put items of clothing belonging to babies, men, women, children, and extra heavy, tall, or short people. Let each child remove an article of clothing and tell who he/she thinks it belongs to and why.
Materials: Various items of clothing, clothes hamper

WHERE DO I WEAR IT?

Tune – "The Farmer In the Dell"
The shirt goes on my arms.
The shirt goes on my arms.
Hi, ho, when I get dressed,
The shirt goes on my arms.
Continue with:
The pants go on my legs.
The socks go on my feet.
The shoes go on my feet.
The hat goes on my head.
The mittens go on my hands. (etc.)
Materials: None

PUT IT IN THE DRAWER

Give each child a shoe box to be a closet or dresser. Cut out or draw pictures of clothing. Mount these pictures on small index cards. Give each child ten to fifteen cards. Also, make a set of cards with a number from one to five on each card. Let the children take turns drawing a card and putting the specified number of clothing items into the closet/dresser. The game continues until all the clothing is gone.
Materials: Shoe boxes, pictures of clothing, index cards, markers, scissors

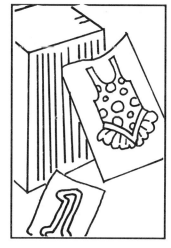

SHIRTS AND JEANS

Using construction paper, cut out ten shirts and ten pairs of jeans with belts. Put a number from one through ten on each belt buckle. Decorate each shirt with one to ten items (five stripes, three circles, etc.). Let the child match shirt to jeans by matching set to number.
Materials: Construction paper, markers or crayons, scissors

MATCH THE CLOTHESLINE
Give students paper clothing items. Hang a number of clothing items on a clothesline. Let the children imitate the pattern using the paper pieces.
Materials: Clothesline, clothing items, clothespins, small paper clothing items

CLOTHES HORSE
Give each child a picture of a horse and ask him/her to draw or design clothes for the horse. Let children show off and describe their horses.
Materials: Picture of horse, crayons, markers, etc.

ZIPPITY DAY
Call on a child to dress a paper doll with the appropriate clothing for the verse of this song:

    Tune – "Zippity Do Da"
    Zippity Do Da,
    Zippity Day.
    I wonder what I should wear today.
    Plenty of _____ (rain) is heading my way.
    Zippity Do Da,
    Zippity Day.

(Change weather condition each time you sing the song.)
Materials: Paper doll with several pieces of seasonal clothing

FASTENERS

PRESS BUTTON

Have each child flatten a ball of clay. Let the children select different shaped buttons and make imprints in the clay. Let the clay dry.
Materials: Clay, buttons

BUTTONS AND BOWS

Draw different-sized bows on a sturdy cloth. Make a different-sized buttonhole in each center. On a separate cloth, attach corresponding-sized buttons. Attach the two cloths by buttoning them together. If desired, this can be secured to a frame.
Materials: Colored markers, buttons of different sizes, optional frame

BUTTONS AND BUTTONHOLES

This is an activity that requires the children to match the two parts of a fastener that go together. Attach a button, hook, half of a snap, part of a shoelace, and part of a zipper to one side of a piece of tagboard. Attach a buttonhole (cut from a shirt), an eye, the other half of a snap, eyelets, and the other half of a zipper to the opposite side of the piece of tagboard. The companion items should not be directly across from each other. Glue one end of a shoestring next to each item on the right side of the board. Punch a small hole next to each item on the other side. The children should put two correct fastener parts together by putting the end of the shoe string through the hole by the correct answer. (See illustration.)
Materials: Fasteners, tagboard, glue, shoestrings

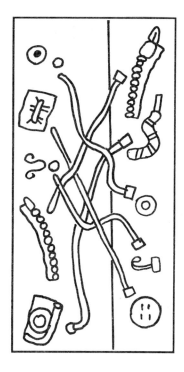

BUTTONS, BUCKLES, AND BOWS – OH, MY!
Have the children put on adult-sized clothes which will require them to button, buckle, and tie. Have two children race and see who can put on all the clothes the fastest and then unbuckle, unbutton, untie, and take them off. While they are doing this, the other children can chant, "Buttons, buckles, and bows – oh, my!"
Materials: Adult-sized clothing

ZIP YOUR LIP
Make a face on an 8" x 10" piece of sturdy cloth. Use large buttons for eyes and nose and a real zipper for the mouth. Attach to an 8" x 10" frame, or make your own frame. Children can practice zipping.
Materials: Large buttons, zipper, 8" x 10" picture frame, sturdy cloth
Variation: Make a clown face.

ZIP, SNAP, BUTTON, AND TIE (A FELT BOARD STORY)
Once upon a time there was a boy named Matt. Matt always liked to do things in a hurry. In the morning he would wake up fast, brush his teeth fast, and even put on his clothes fast! In fact, he would put on his clothes so fast, he would forget to button his shirt, zip his pants, snap the top, and tie his shoes. Then, as he would run outside, what do you think would happen? His pants would fall down, his shirt would fly open, and he would lose his shoes! Then, he would have to start all over again, pulling up his pants, buttoning his shirt, and putting on his shoes. This took so much more time, and Matt wanted to play. This made Matt cry. One day, Matt's mom saw him crying. She taught him a song to remember to zip, button, snap, and tie! She sang:
> Tune – "This Old Man"
> Zip, button, snap, and tie...
> And I will tell you why...
> If you zip, button, snap, and tie,
> Your clothes will stay on —
> And you won't cry.

When Matt woke up in the morning, he would sing his song and remember to zip, button, snap, and tie. (During the story, put clothes on the Matt doll and make them "fly off" at appropriate times.)
Materials: Felt board, felt boy, and felt clothing items

FIND A FASTENER

Collect pictures of fasteners or use real fasteners attached to cards. Let the children select a card, identify the fastener, and search the room to find another similar fastener (button – buttons on a coat, blouse, puppet, etc.). For more obscure fasteners (hook and eye), be sure items with the fasteners are located around the room.

Materials: Pictures of fasteners, real fasteners, items of clothing, etc., that have the same fasteners as the stimulus cards.

BUTTON BANK

Cut a small slot in the top of a box. Let the children sort different sized buttons to fit in the box. The children should explain why remaining buttons did not fit, e.g., too large.

Materials: Shoe box or margarine tub, various-sized buttons

BUTTON ORDER

Cut out a large construction paper shirt. Cut out buttons 1 1/2" around. Punch one, two, three, or four button holes in each button. Let the children place the buttons in order on the shirt.

Materials: Construction paper, markers, scissors

61

SHOES, SOCKS, & FEET

SHOE SHAPES
Using markers, trace the outlines of each shoe in a separate shoe box. The children should match the shoe pictures to the appropriate shoe box.

Materials: Shoe picture cutouts (rain boot, cowboy boot, tennis shoe, sandal, slipper, little girl's strap shoe, skate, etc.), construction paper, shoe boxes, markers, scissors

THESE SHOES HAVE "SOLE"
Tape a number to the bottom of each child's shoe. Tell the children they need to remember that number. When it is their turn, they should stamp the floor in place the same number of times which corresponds to the number on the bottom of their shoe. The rest of the children should count the stamps and then check the number.

Materials: Paper, marker, tape

Variation: Give a number to each child. Have each child stamp in order – 1,2,3...

WHOSE SHOES ARE THESE?
Make a game by gluing a picture of a man, woman, child, and baby across the top of a file folder. Cut out catalog pictures of different shoes and socks. Mount these pictures on index cards. The children sort the cards by matching shoes and socks to the person who wears them.

Materials: File folders, catalogs, index cards, glue

SHOES AND SOCKS

Tune – "Love And Marriage"
Shoes and socks,
Shoes and socks,
Go together like keys and locks,
Any kind of weather,
Shoes and socks can go together.
Materials: None

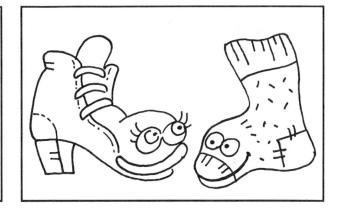

THE SHOE ZOO

Trace around one foot of each child. Let him/her make it into a zoo animal by adding a head, tail, legs, etc.
Materials: Paper, crayons or markers

STRIPES

Draw and cut out a variety of tennis shoes and socks. Draw stripes on the sides of the shoes (one to five stripes). On the top of the socks, also draw one to five stripes. Let the children match the socks to the shoes by matching the numbers of stripes on the shoe and the sock (two stripes on a shoe – two on a sock).
Materials: Construction paper, markers, scissors

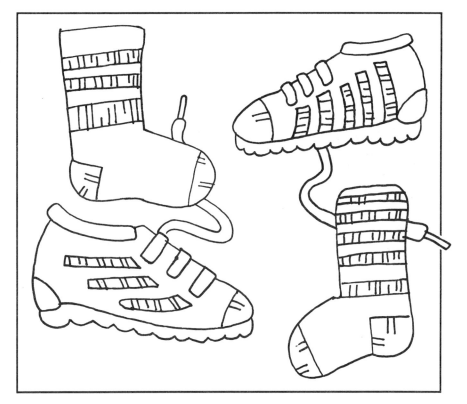

HOW WOULD I WALK?
Talk about what you wear on your feet (shoes, slippers, sandals, boots, etc.). Have these items available for the children to try on and walk in. Then talk about them wearing such things as a pan, paper sack, shoe box, roller skate, helmet, pail, etc., on their feet. Let each child try to walk with an "absurd" item on his/her foot. Supervise closely to avoid falling, etc. Have the children describe how it feels to walk in a pan, box, etc. Also, have the children suggest names of these items if we wore them on our feet, e.g., a "sacky" shoe.
Materials: Footwear, other items to wear as footwear

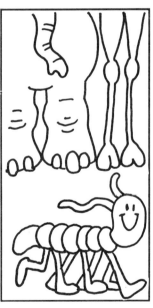

MANY FEET/FEW FEET
Discuss many and few with the group. Divide the children into two groups – one with a few children, the other with many children. Tell the children that when you give a direction with "many feet" that the larger group should follow the direction. If you give a direction with "few feet," the smaller group follows the direction.

    Many feet, many feet, hop, hop, hop.
    Many feet, many feet, run, run, run.
    Few feet, many feet, walk for fun!
    Many feet, many feet, walk for fun!

Vary directions.
Materials: None

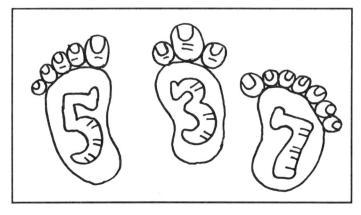

TOES, TOES, TOES
Cut out one to ten feet without toes. Put a number on each foot. Cut out a variety of toes – big and little. Let the children attach toes to feet to match numbers to sets.
Materials: Paper, markers, paste, glue, construction paper

HATS

WHOSE HAT IS IT?

Assemble a variety of real or paper hats representing different occupations (cowboy, fireman, policeman, construction worker, football player, nurse, baseball player). Tell the children a riddle about each hat, and let them try to guess whose hat it is. Example: I ride a truck and help put out fires. Which hat do I wear? Or, I ride horses and live on a ranch. Which hat do I wear?

Materials: Real or construction paper hats, scissors

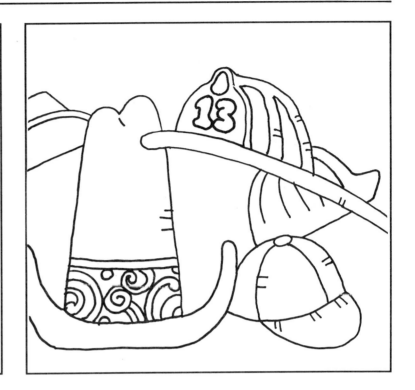

THE CHILD WITH TOO MANY HATS

Read the story, *Caps For Sale*. Have the children pretend that paper plates are caps. As one child stands and balances, the teacher or another student places "caps" on his/her head. The rest of the class counts to see how many caps are being balanced.

Materials: The story, *Caps For Sale*, paper plates

STACK THE HATS

Cut out two sets of graduated sizes of hats from felt. Mix up the sizes of each set of hats on the felt board. Then call upon two children to race and see who can put their hats in order from the largest to the smallest hat.

Materials: Felt, flannel board, scissors

HATS

Tune – "London Bridge"
Cowboys wear cowboy hats,
   cowboy hats, cowboy hats.
Cowboys wear cowboy hats,
   when they go to work.
Baseball players – baseball caps
Football players – football helmets
Policemen – policemen's hats
Materials: Various hats

PASS THE HAT

Let the children find small items that will fit into a hat. The hat is passed around a circle, and each child says, "I have a (toy car) for someone." He/she puts it into the hat. After everyone has put something into the hat, each child takes something out and remembering who put it into the hat, thanks him/her.
Materials: A hat, various small items
Variation: Everyone finds items that are the same color or shape or items which begin with a certain sound.

IN THE HAT

Put numerals in one hat and a large quantity of identical items (blocks, bottle caps, pennies, etc.) into another hat. The child should pull a numeral from one hat and a corresponding number of items from the other hat.
Materials: Two hats, numbered cards, numerous identical items

HOLIDAY SPIRITS

BELLS

RING THE BELLS
Using a safety pin, attach one bell to each child's pant leg, sleeve, shirt front, waistband, and to the back of the child's shirt/pants. The children should "play" a song by moving a specific body part, thus ringing the bell. Let the children take turns being the "conductor" and naming the body part to move.
Materials: Bells, safety pins

RING-A-LING
Provide the students with a variety of colored bells. Sing the song, and have the students holding the color bell named in the song stand up and ring their bell. Change the color of the bell in the verse of the song each time.

> Tune – "Farmer In The Dell"
> Ring-a-ling-a-ling.
> Oh, hear the ____ bells ring.
> To tell the world it's Christmastime.
> Ring-a-ling-a-ling.

Materials: Variety of colored bells

THREE BELLS
Cut three bells out of construction paper – one large, one medium, one small. Using a file folder or a large piece of tagboard, make ten to twelve small doors. Do this by cutting along three sides of a small drawn square. On each door glue a small picture, number, color, shape, etc., (whatever concept you are currently working on). Cut out three circles – these are the clappers. One should be large, one medium-sized, and one small. Place these circles behind three different doors. Read the following story:
"Once upon a time there were three bells. They were very sad this holiday time because they had misplaced their clappers, and they couldn't decorate Santa's sleigh if they couldn't ring. They looked and looked for their clappers, but they just couldn't find them. Would the boys and girls like to help?"
The children look for the clappers by suggesting a door to open (behind the red one, behind the apple, etc.). If the children find the clapper, they have to attach it to the same-sized bell. Continue play until all the clappers have been found; then hide the clappers again.
Materials: Construction paper, file folders

SILVER BELLS
Write the numerals from one to ten on paper bells. Provide the students with a bowl of silver bells (foil wrapped chocolates), and have them put the appropriate quantity of silver bells on each paper bell.
Materials: Ten paper bells, marker, foil wrapped chocolates

WHERE'S THE MOUSE?
Cut out several different-colored paper bells. Cut out a mouse. Tell the children that the mouse likes to hide under a bell. Place the mouse under one of the bells. The children should visually track as you move the bells around. Choose a child to find the mouse.
Materials: Paper bells, paper mouse, construction paper, scissors
Variation: Make all the bells the same color. This will make the task more difficult and will require the children to follow as the mouse is placed and moved.

I HEARD THE BELLS
Have the children count the number of times the bell rings. Have them choose a number and ring the bell the chosen number of times.
Materials: Bells

RING THE NAME BELL

Place bells in front of the children. Child A rings bells and says:

> Ringing bells for Steven.
> Ringing bells for Steven.
> These bells are ringing just for Steven.

Steven then decides for whom he will ring the bells. Continue play until all the children's names have been used and each has had a turn to ring the bells.

Materials: Bells

BELL JEWELRY & HAIR ORNAMENTS

Have a large selection of different-sized bells and different-sized colored bells for the children to make jewelry and hair ornaments. Suggestions include: bracelets, necklaces, ankle bracelets, barrettes, headbands. The children can keep their creation or give it as a gift.

Materials: Different sizes and different colors of bells, heavyweight string or bendable wire, plain barrettes, plastic headbands, craft glue

BELL SORTING

Purchase different-sized jingle bells – about eight to ten of each size. Mix all the bells in a bowl/box. Let the children sort the bells by putting the same-sized bells together. Activity continues until all the bells are sorted.

Materials: Different-sized bells, large bowl or box

ELVES

SANTA HAD SOME LITTLE ELVES
Tune – "Mary Had A Little Lamb"
Santa had some little elves, little elves, little elves
Santa had some little elves,
Who made toys for girls and boys.

They worked all night and worked all day, worked all day,
   worked all day,
They worked all night and worked all day,
To bring kids Christmas joy!
Materials: None

WE'RE THE ELVES
Tune – "Three Blind Mice"
We're the elves,
We're the elves.
We work hard!
We work hard!
We make all the trucks, the cars, and the trains.
We make all the dolls, the bikes, and the planes.
We feed the reindeer that pull the sleigh.
We're the elves!
Materials: None

THIS LITTLE ELF
Paste the pictures of Santa, a house, a toy, and three elves onto different tongue depressors or on the children's fingers.
   This little elf went to Santa.
   This little elf went home.
   This little elf just worked, worked, worked,
until all the toys were done.
Materials: Pictures of Santa, house, toy, three elves; tongue depressors; glue/tape

ELF SHOES

Make "elf" shoes using adult-sized green stockings. Stuff cotton, material scraps, etc., snuggly into the tip of the stocking. Form this into a point, and secure with a rubber band (place rubber band 2 to 3 inches up from the toe area). You may want to sew bells to the cuffs. Have the children wear the shoes and prance around like little elves.

Materials: Large green stocking, stuffing materials, rubber bands

SANTA ELF

One day, Little Elf said, "I want to be Santa. Santa wears a red suit." So he put on a red suit (red pajamas). "Santa wears a red hat," he said. So he put on a red hat (red top hat). "Santa wears boots; I'll put on boots!" (Orange boots.) "Santa has a beard," he said. So he put on a beard (black beard). Then he went to the children and said, "I'm Santa Claus. Hee, hee, hee!" The children said, "You're not Santa!" How did the children know Little Elf was not Santa?

Materials: A skinny, tiny elf; red pajamas; red top hat; orange boots; black beard; optional – picture of Santa

SANTA'S HELPER

One adult or child is Santa. This person can wear a pretend beard, a red construction paper hat, and/or a red coat. All the other children are elves. Santa asks the elves to help him/her do something (hammer, feed the reindeer, wash the sleigh, fill his/her sack, etc.). The children who are elves act out the scene.

Materials: Cotton, construction paper, red coat, any other prop desired

ORNAMENTS

MESH ORNAMENTS
Cut mesh bags similar to those in which onions are packed, into 6 or 7 inch square pieces. Fill the center with styrofoam packing pieces, gather at the top, and tie with a ribbon.
Materials: Different-colored mesh bags, styrofoam pieces, ribbon

ORNAMENT OUTLINES
Cut out and laminate a variety of different-shaped ornaments (circle, oval, triangular, cone, tree, star, etc.). On green tagboard, draw and cut out a large Christmas tree. Using a dark marker, trace all the ornaments on the tree. Let the children match the ornament to its outline.
Materials: Construction paper, tagboard, marker, scissors

BALLOON ORNAMENTS
Blow up balloons to use as ornaments. Have one child pretend to be a Christmas tree, and let the other children use tape to attach the "ornaments" to the "tree."
Materials: Various-colored balloons, tape

HOUSE ORNAMENT

Cut out large Christmas trees. Draw ten to fifteen circles on the trees where ornaments will be placed. Cut out same-sized circles (ornaments) from various colors of construction paper. Cut out ten extra ornaments. Draw mice on five of these. Put all the ornaments face-down in a pile. The children should take turns picking an ornament for their tree. If the mouse is chosen, that child must clear his/her ornament(s) from his/her tree and begin again to fill the tree with ornaments.

Materials: Paper tree and ornaments, marker/crayon, scissors

ORNAMENT PATTERN

Cut out and laminate circle, square, and triangular-shaped ornaments which are all the same color. Cut out a large green tree. Let the children follow a specific pattern as they place the ornaments on the tree (circle, square, triangle, circle, square – or triangle, triangle, circle, circle, triangle...). The complexity of the pattern will depend on the abilities of the children. The pattern can be given orally to the children, or they can copy a predrawn pattern.

Materials: Construction paper (or tagboard), scissors

ROLL CANDY PERSON ORNAMENT

Provide a roll of candy for each child. Let each child decorate his/her roll candy person as he/she wishes. Suggestions include: styrofoam head glued on top with small stars or glitter for eyes and a red marker mouth. Glue pipe cleaners to roll of candy on sides for arms and at bottom for legs. Or, a piece of yarn can be pulled through the roll candy with a needle for the arms and yarn pieces glued at the bottom for legs. Stick an ornament hanger in the top of the styrofoam head for hanging.

Materials: Roll candy, small styrofoam balls, yarn, pipe cleaners, markers, glue, needle (for teacher uses only)

Variation: Let children make roll candy animal ornaments.

REINDEER

TACTILE REINDEER
Cut a large reindeer's head out of tagboard or cardboard. Include a large rack of antlers on top of the deer's head. Cover each of the antler points with a different texture (felt, sandpaper, netting, flannel, self-adhesive paper, etc.). Attach the same materials to small rectangles. Cover each child's eyes, and give him/her one of the rectangles. Using touch only, the child should try to match the texture he/she feels on the rectangle with one of the antler points.
Materials: Tagboard or cardboard, various textured materials, glue, scissors

REINDEER TOSS
Cut a reindeer's head (without antlers) out of heavy cardboard. Attach the reindeer to the edge of a table (tape or tack). (The head should extend several inches above the edge of the table.) Using masking tape, attach two paper towel rolls to the reindeer's head. Rest the ends of the paper towels on the table's surface. (These are the antlers, and they should be several inches apart.) Make small rings out of heavy tagboard, oatmeal lids, or purchase small plastic rings. The children should stand a short distance from the reindeer's head and toss the rings at the antlers.
Materials: Tagboard or cardboard, paper towel rolls, oatmeal lids/ small plastic rings, table, masking tape, tacks

REINDEER TRACKS
You will need snow on the ground for this! Have the children put fists inside paper cups. Have them make reindeer tracks in the snow.
Materials: Snow, paper cups
Variation: Bring snow inside and put it into a pan.

MAKE A REINDEER

Paint 16 ounce round oatmeal boxes and small paper plates brown. Poke four clothespins in the bottom of the box as the legs. Add deer facial features and antlers (pipe cleaners) to the paper plate. Attach the paper plate and the tail.

Materials: Oatmeal box, small paper plate, brown paint, construction paper, pipe cleaners

DEER ME

Child A pretends to be a hungry deer. He/she goes from "animal" to "animal" looking for food. (Other students pick the animal they want to pretend to be.)

    Child A: What kind of animal are you?
    Child B: I'm a _____ (squirrel).
    Child A: I'm hungry. What do you have to eat?
    Child B: I have some _____ (nuts). Do you want some?
    Child A: Yes, thank-you.

Materials: Pictures of animals, animal foods (nuts, worms, fish, meat, etc.), deer antlers optional

REINDEER ANTLERS

Have three or four deer faces pasted to paper. Let the children use a variety of materials to make "different" antlers (feathers, straw, paper strips, plastic strips, ribbons, etc.).

Materials: Construction paper, three or four faces of reindeer, various materials for antlers

WREATHS

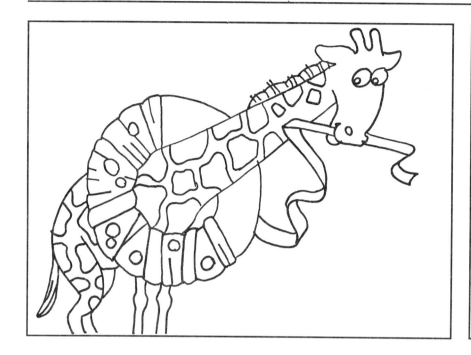

WRAP THE WREATH
Cut out circular pieces of cardboard (like dough-nuts). Cut green garbage bags into strips. Fasten the beginning of the strip onto the board, and wrap around to cover the cardboard. Decorate with paper berries.
Materials: Cardboard wreath, green garbage bags, tape, paper berries, scissors

BOTTLE CAP WREATH
Cut out various-sized circles from sturdy paper. On each circle, write a number. Have the children glue the corresponding number of bottle caps around the edge of the circle to form a wreath. Spray-paint green.
Materials: Bottle caps, sturdy paper, spray paint, glue, scissors

MATCH THE WREATH
Cut out construction paper doors and wreaths. Put numbers or letters on the doors and on the wreaths. Let the children match wreaths to the door with the same letter/number. (Can be attached with a removable adhesive.)
Materials: Paper wreaths, paper doors, scissors, removable adhesive

WREATH BERRIES

Cut out wreaths. Put a numeral at the top and laminate. Let the children dip fingers in red paint to make corresponding number of berries.

Materials: Laminated wreaths, finger paint, construction paper, scissors

Variation: Use plastic counting chips instead of finger paint. Do not laminate the wreaths. Let the children keep the wreaths they make.

COUNT THE BERRIES

Cut one to ten rectangles out of tagboard. Attach a small magnet to each door. Put a number on each door using a marker. Arrange the doors on a surface so that the numbers are in order from one to ten. Cut ten small wreaths out of green tagboard. Attach a small magnet to the back of each wreath. Color, paint, or glue one to ten red berries on each wreath. (Do not duplicate any sets.) Let the children match sets to the appropriate number by attaching wreaths to doors. For example, the wreath with five berries should be placed on the door with the number five.

Materials: Tagboard, markers, magnets, scissors, glue

WREATHS ON THE DOOR

Cut one to ten rectangles out of brown felt. These are the doors. Place the doors on a small felt board. Write a number on each door using a dark marker. Cut a number of small wreaths out of green felt. Let the children attach wreaths to a door to match the number on the door (for number 3, put on 3 wreaths).

Materials: Brown and green felt, felt board, marker, scissors

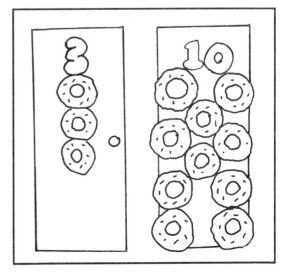

SCARECROWS

LET'S BE A SCARECROW
Have the children bring old pants, shirts, and hats to school. Provide straw, strips of newspaper, yarn, facial makeup, etc. Encourage the children to help each other turn into scarecrows.
Materials: Straw, strips of newspaper, facial makeup, children's clothing from home

WHAT KIND OF HAT?
Draw a large scarecrow or make one by stuffing clothing with newspapers. Cut out or collect an assortment of hats. "Try" each hat on the scarecrow to find the one that would be most appropriate. You may want to prompt creative thinking from the children by asking, "What kind of scarecrow would wear a hat like this?" (Baseball cap.) Answer, "One who likes baseball!"
Materials: Scarecrow, variety of hats

MAKE A SCARECROW
Cut out felt or paper pieces of a scarecrow (hat, head, shirt, pants, two sleeves, two shoes). Give each child one set of scarecrow pieces. The children should put together or "build" a scarecrow as they respond correctly to different questions. Depending on the level of the children, questions could include identifying body parts, naming colors, identifying letters or numbers, etc. Continue the game until each child has built an entire scarecrow. (Always start with the headpiece.)
Materials: Construction paper, scissors, markers

SCARECROW CONTEST

Provide the children with old doll or infant clothing, or have them bring these items from home. Have the children stuff the clothing with newspaper to make the scarecrow bodies. Stuff lunch bags with newspaper for the heads, and attach to the bodies. Have the children glue on paper or scraps (yarn, buttons, etc.) to make the face. Have a scarecrow parade, and let the children decide what is funny about each scarecrow.

Materials: Scraps (yarn, buttons, etc.), lunch bags, glue, doll or infant clothing

SCARECROW BOOK

Cut out five identically-shaped scarecrows. Attach them together in book fashion. Decorate each scarecrow with buttons, yarn, markers, wallpaper scraps, etc. Make sure that each scarecrow is different.

Materials: Buttons, straw, markers, wallpaper samples, scissors, paper

Variation: Cut out only the hat, hair, and face.

CROW MATH

Make a scarecrow using tongue depressors for arms. Cut out and attach ten paper crows to ten clip-on clothespins. Attach the crows to the scarecrow's arms using whatever math concepts are appropriate for your class. (Two crows on one arm and three on another equals _____ . Six crows were on the scarecrow. Two flew away. _____ were left.)

Materials: Clip-on clothespins, crows, scarecrows, tongue depressors, paper, scissors

PILGRIMS

PILGRIM PLAYTIME
Explain to the children that pilgrim children did not have toys like the ones we have today. Give the children old-fashioned toys such as a stick and a ball, dirt in a cup, acorns and a cup. Let children have "playtime" the old-fashioned way.
Materials: "Natural" toys such as a stick, ball, acorns, etc.

PILGRIM AND INDIAN DANCE
Dress half of the children as pilgrims and half as Indians. Form two lines with the pilgrims facing the Indians. The Indian and pilgrim at the end of each line join hands and walk together through the line while everyone sings:

> Tune – "The More We Get Together"
> We can walk together.
> The two of us,
> The two of us.
> We can walk together,
> The pilgrim and the Indian.

When the first pair reaches the end of the line, the next pair starts. Let children suggest different activities – run, hop, skip, etc.

THE BIG SWITCH
Cut out two paper dolls – a pilgrim and an Indian. Cut out typical clothing for each. Place the wrong clothing on each paper doll. Call on two children to switch the clothing back and forth by requesting items until the Indian and pilgrim are wearing their own clothes.
Materials: Paper dolls, clothing, scissors

PILGRIM HATS

Make several pilgrim hats with some similarities and some differences. Have the children identify similarities and differences. (Vary size, shape, colors, etc.)
Materials: Premade pilgrim hats

PILGRIM, PILGRIM, WHERE'S YOUR HAT?

Have the children stand in a circle. Choose one child to be the pilgrim and stand in the middle. Blindfold this child. Let the other children in the circle pass the hat to each other saying:

Pilgrim, pilgrim, where's your hat?
We've passed it around the circle.
Now you try to get it back.

The children stop passing the hat when the poem is completed. The child who has the hat at this point hides it behind his back. The pilgrim tries to guess who has the hat.
Materials: Pilgrim hat

THANKSGIVING DINNER

Make Indian and pilgrim hats for the children, and act out the following sequence story:

Once upon a time, a pilgrim boy and girl decided to have a dinner and they invited their friends the Indians and other pilgrims. After they invited their friends to the dinner, they went hunting for a turkey. Then they cooked the turkey. Everyone sat down to eat.
Materials: Pilgrim and Indian hats, additional props

INDIANS

INDIAN, INDIAN
Tune – "Brown Bear, Brown Bear"
Indian, Indian, what do you do?
I ride my horse, and I paddle my canoe.
Indian, Indian, what do you see?
I see my house that's a little tepee.
Indian, Indian, what do you eat?
I eat yellow corn and juicy turkey meat.
Indian, Indian, what do you say?
I say, "How!" and "Have a nice day!"

SEE THE INDIANS
Tune – "Mary Had A Little Lamb"
See the Indians shoot the arrow
shoot the arrow
shoot the arrow.
See the Indians shoot the arrow
to catch some food.
(See the Indians row the canoes, ride the horses, beat the drums, etc.)

MATCH THE PATTERN
Cut out six to ten different-colored feathers and attach them to a headband. This is the model pattern. Let children cut out their own headband and colored feathers and arrange the feathers in the same order as the pattern.
Materials: Paper, scissors
Variation: Use the same-colored paper for the feathers – vary the pattern on the feathers (one with squares, one with stars, one with triangles, etc.)

INSIDE THE TEPEE

Collect action pictures from magazines and glue two to three pictures to a piece of paper. Let the children cut brown construction paper tepees with doors. Put this over a magazine picture. Let the children open the "tepee" door and describe what is happening inside.

Materials: Brown construction paper, magazine pictures, glue, scissors

TOTEM POLE TUMBLES

Have children paint various boxes or containers which have lids. Glue one large magazine picture on each side, or have children draw pictures. Let the children stack the boxes on top of each other building a totem pole. Have children name the items going up or down the totem pole.

Materials: Oatmeal or other boxes, paint, glue, magazine pictures

Variation: Number totem poles and stack them in order.

FILL THE TEPEE

Cut out brown construction paper tepees and paste to a piece of paper. Cut and write numerals on doors that open. Let the children draw the specified amount of drums, corn, etc., inside the tepee.

Materials: Brown construction paper, paste, markers or crayons, scissors

INDIAN CHIEF

Each Indian comes to the chief and tells what he did to help (made a tepee, killed a buffalo, planted corn, etc.). The chief gives each a feather for helping.

Materials: Chief headdress, feathers

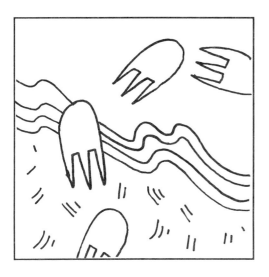

TRACK THE BEAR

Set up a forest scene (table – bridge; draw a lake on the floor, etc.). Choose one child to be the Indian brave. While the Indian brave is "sleeping," the teacher or another student lays down bear tracks. When the brave awakens, he follows the tracks and tells where the bear traveled (under the bridge, around the lake, etc.).

Materials: Bear footprints

INDIAN FEATHERS

Make one to ten headbands and write a number from one to ten on the headbands. Make small loops or pockets on the headband into which the feathers can be inserted. Make the same number of loops on each headband. Cut out the number of feathers as needed for the activity. Let the children put the correct number of feathers in each headband to match the number on the headband.

Materials: Paper

TURKEYS

MAKING A TURKEY

Use a styrofoam ball for the turkey's body. Trim plastic leaves to look like feathers. Poke these into one end of the ball. Use two larger leaves as side wings. Use the "vine" part of the leaves (plastic strips) as legs. Cut a construction paper head. You may want to paint the styrofoam ball.

Materials: Styrofoam ball, plastic leaves, construction paper, scissors

ADD A FEATHER

Cut out a large turkey body to be hung on the wall. Glue removable adhesive strips along the tail line. Cut colored feathers and glue strips on these. Give each child a feather. As the child identifies the color, numeral, letter, etc., on the feather, let him "stick" it on the giant turkey. (This turkey can be used daily to reinforce concepts or themes covered that day.)

Materials: Cutout paper turkey (laminated or poster board), removable adhesive, glue, cutout feathers (laminated or poster board), scissors

TURKEY TALK

The teacher is the turkey and sounds out a variety of gobble patterns which the children try to imitate. Patterns should start off simple and increase in complexity by varying lengths, durations, intonations, rate, volume, and pitch.

Materials: None

TURKEY SOUP
Have the children cut out a large construction paper soup pot. Have them paste a paper turkey in the pot and look through magazines or loose pictures to add any items they would like in their turkey soup.

Materials: Construction paper, magazine pictures, scissors, glue/paste

TURKEY FEATHERS
Cut out a number of turkey bodies without feathers on the tail. Glue a picture on each turkey representing phonic sounds (baby, dog, horse, etc.). Cut out a variety of feathers and write a consonant on each feather. These consonants should correspond to previously selected pictures. Turn all feathers facedown on a table or the floor in front of the children. Then, let the children take turns selecting a feather, identifying the sound, and matching it to the correct turkey. Glue or tape the feathers to the turkey. Continue until all the feathers are attached to a turkey.

Materials: Cutout turkeys and feathers, markers, pictures, tape or glue, scissors

Variation: Use numerals and sets.

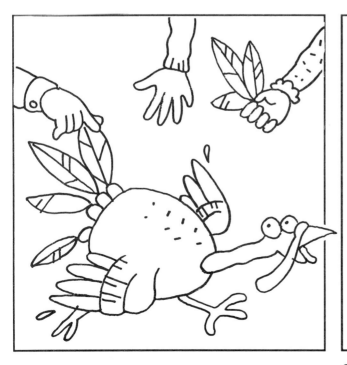

PLUCK THE TURKEY
Cut out ten paper feathers using all the basic colors (red, green, white, blue, yellow, orange, brown, black, purple, pink). Attach the feathers to a large turkey. Let the children take turns plucking one of the feathers off the turkey. Then let them go on a scavenger hunt and find an item that matches the color of their feather.

Materials: Colored paper feathers, large cutout turkey, scissors, tape

Variation: Have all the children search for one item the color of the plucked feather.

USEFUL ITEMS

OBJECT FUNCTIONS

MUSICAL OBJECTS
Place a variety of common objects evenly spaced around a circle. Have the children walk around the objects as music is played. When the music stops, let the children grab an object and tell the function of it. An object is taken away with each round.
Materials: Record player, record, group of common objects

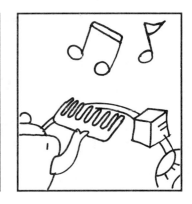

LET'S PRETEND
Give each child a wooden block. Suggest or have a child suggest an action, e.g., washing. Let the children pretend that the block is a bar of soap and use it to wash their hands. Suggest and act out other actions.
Materials: Wooden blocks
Variation: Do not use actual objects. Let the children pretend they have the object needed to complete the action.

FOOTPRINTS
Glue pictures of objects on cutout footprints. Place the footprints on the floor/ground. Give one, two, or three step directions. For example, "Step on the object that you use to brush your teeth and then on the object that you use to write with."
Materials: Pictures of objects, cutout footprints, glue
Variation: Use handprints secured to the wall.
Variation II: Use two different objects that have the same function - cup and glass. Place feet on objects you drink from.

FURNITURE

TV TOAST
Cut the crust off a slice of bread. Use a can of pressurized cheese to draw a square for the TV screen. Add raisins for knobs. If applicable, the children can draw a face, house, tree, etc., on the TV.
Materials: Slices of bread, pressurized can of cheese, raisins, knife
Variation: Use a tiny brush dipped in milk colored with food coloring to make TV screen. Toast and eat.

WHAT GOES WITH WHAT!
Find pictures of furniture (bed, table, dresser, etc.) in magazines, catalogs, newspaper ads, etc. Use a file folder as the game board. Glue the pictures on the file folder allowing enough space to place game cards. Depending on the size of the furniture pictures, this could mean two or three pictures on each side of the file folder. Using a dark marker, mark off spaces for each furniture item. Also, find pictures of objects that go with the original pieces of furniture selected. For example, sheets and a pillow go with a bed; plates and utensils go with the table, etc. Cut out and glue pictures of these items to index cards. Let the children play the game by placing pictures of objects that go with the items of furniture next to that piece of furniture on the board. The game ends when all the cards are correctly distributed.
Materials: File folders, magazines, catalogs, newspaper ads, index cards, scissors, glue

FURNITURE GROUPS
Find pictures of a variety of furniture in magazines, catalogs, and sales ads. Cut out the pictures and glue them onto index cards. Laminate if possible. During small group sessions, let the children sort cards on the basis of:

    Rooms the furniture is generally found in.

    Things you can sit on, lie on, etc.

    Things that are hard/soft.

    Things that we can set a glass of water on.

    Materials the items are made of.

Let the children suggest different ways to group the furniture.
Materials: Index cards, magazines, catalogs, newspaper ads, scissors, glue

THREE BEARS' FURNITURE
Tell the children the story of *Goldilocks And The Three Bears*. After the story, talk about the furniture described in the story – chairs and beds. Have available soft, hard, and tiny chairs and soft, hard, and tiny beds. Let the children take turns sitting in the chairs and lying on the beds and pretend they are Goldilocks. They can also recite the dialogue or describe in their own words how the different items of furniture "feel."

Materials: Papa Bear's chair – large wooden chair
Mama's chair – a beanbag chair
Baby's chair – a small rocker
Papa's bed – a large board covered with a sheet
Mama's bed – several quilts on top of an air mattress
Baby's bed – a small cot

CHAIR LEGS
Talk about how furniture has "legs." Compare to all the other things that have legs – people, elephants, dogs, cats, horses, birds, etc. Make a variety of legs (animal, people, etc.) to attach to a chair seat. Have the children think of names for the chairs.

Materials: Paper, markers, tape or glue

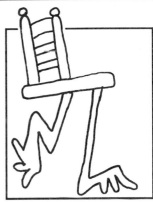

BODY FURNITURE
Help the children position their bodies as they pretend to be different pieces of furniture. For example, a child could pretend to be a chair by squatting down or sitting cross-legged on the floor and holding out his/her arms. Several children could sit next to each other with an arm around each other's shoulders as the two end children extend one arm out as they pretend to be a couch. Let the children extend on hands and knees as they pretend to be a table. Let your imagination go. Have the children try to guess what piece of furniture the others are. After the children have pretended to be furniture using their bodies, give them a pile of wooden blocks and let them create furniture.

TOOLS

TOOL SONG
Act out motions using real, toy, or make-believe tools.
Tune – "Mary Had A Little Lamb"
I use a hammer to pound, pound, pound,
Pound, pound, pound
Pound, pound, pound.
I use a hammer to pound, pound, pound,
To pound in a nail.

I use a saw to cut, cut, cut,
Cut, cut, cut
Cut, cut, cut.
I use a saw to cut, cut, cut,
Cut a piece of wood.
(I use a screwdriver to turn, turn, turn,...
Turn a screw around, etc.)
(I use a drill to make a hole, make a hole, make a hole,...
Make a great big hole.)
Materials: real or toy tools

REPAIRPERSON'S BELT
Have each student make a repairperson's belt. Cut a 12 inch piece of paper with squares to tape on as pockets. Punch holes on each end and tie yarn for attaching it. Have the children color and cut out tools to put in the pockets.
Materials: Construction paper, crayons, scissors, tape, yarn

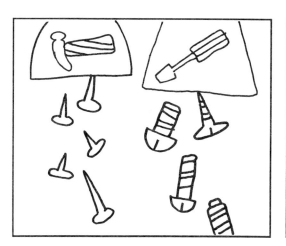

TOOL TOGETHERS
Paste pictures of either hammers or screwdrivers on containers (cans, butter tubs, etc.). Put a numeral on each container. Provide screws and nails which the children count and sort into the proper containers.
Materials: Containers, pictures of tools, screws, nails
Variation: Eliminate numbers

THE TOOLBOX

Fill a toolbox with common plastic tools. Put in some items that are not tools such as a banana, a doll, a sock, etc. Talk about the repairperson who went to work on the house. When he/she opened his/her toolbox, he/she was surprised! Have the children sort through, deciding what items are tools and which are not.

Materials: Toolbox, plastic tools, other objects which are not tools

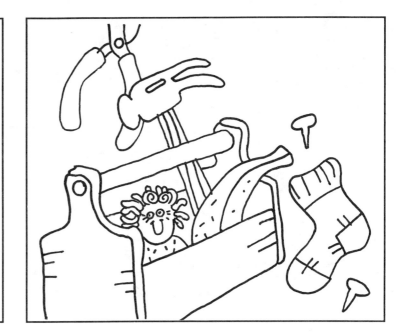

POUND THE HAMMER

Give each child a wooden or plastic hammer. The teacher or one child pounds a specific number of times on a hard surface. The other children should try to match the pattern.

Materials: Wooden or plastic hammers

PUT THE TOOLS AWAY

Place small plastic/metal hooks at various places on a large piece of pegboard. Draw, cut out, and laminate pictures of various tools. Punch a hole at the top of the pictures. Have the children hang the tools at various places on the board (top, bottom, middle, between, etc.).

Materials: Pegboard, hooks, construction paper

VEHICLES

WHAT DO YOU SEE?
Ask half of the class to dress up in a variety of clothing styles (mother, father, police officer, etc.). Give each of the other children a different-colored vehicle. Make a road on the floor with chalk, tape, or blocks. Have the children who are dressed up sit on the side of the road to watch the children push their cars down the road one at a time. Call upon one of the dressed-up children by saying the following rhyme:

Mother, Mother, what do you see?(Or.)
Police officer, police officer, what do you see?

The child responds by naming the color of the vehicle coming.

I see a red car going down the street. (Or.)
I see a yellow truck going down the street.

Materials: Dress-up clothes; toy vehicles; chalk, tape, or blocks.

WHAT'S WRONG?
On a flannel or magnetic board, display a scene that includes a lake/river, road, sky, clouds, railroad tracks, pasture, mountain, house, and other buildings. Make the scene as elaborate or as simple as you wish. Cut out pictures of different transportation items (car, truck, bus, boat, plane, train, etc.). Place these items on the board in incorrect places (put the car in the lake, the train in the sky, etc.). Display the scene to the children. Have the children suggest what is wrong with the scene and how it might be corrected. Talk about why the scene is "funny."
Materials: Paper or felt, flannel board, magnetic board, tape, scissors

MR. MECHANIC
Draw a set of four to six cars of varying sizes on pieces of construction paper. Give each child one of the cars and a corresponding set of wheels of varying sizes. Tell the children they are the mechanics and must glue wheels on the cars and sort the wheels to find the right sizes for each car.
Materials: Construction paper, glue, scissors

BOX VEHICLES

Collect large cardboard boxes. Have the children paint these boxes a solid color – yellow bus, blue car, red caboose, silver/gray truck, white van. Cut out wheels and a windshield, and attach to the box. Cut two large footholes in the front for the children to stick their legs out of as they pretend to press the pedals. Use a paper plate as the steering wheel.

Materials: Large cardboard boxes, paint, paintbrushes, construction paper, paper plate, scissors

RAZY CARS

The children should cut out a variety of shapes – two rectangles, four circles, two squares, and three triangles. (If the children are unable to cut out these shapes individually, distribute precut shapes to them.) Explain to the children that their job is to make a new car, boat, train, etc. Let the children arrange their shapes to make a unique transportation item. Encourage and guide the children to make sure the shapes touch each other to complete the vehicle. Glue the vehicle pieces to a sheet of paper and display.

Materials: Paper, scissors, glue

Variation: If you have access to woodworking tools and materials, or if you have access to a woodworking class, perhaps you could have some of the designs made into wooden vehicles for the children to play with.

VEHICLE SONG

    Tune – "Mary Had A Little Lamb"
    The tugboat floats in the water, in the water, in the water.
    The tugboat floats in the water, toot, toot, toot!

    The shiny car drives on the road, on the road, on the road.
    The shiny car drives on the road, beep, beep, beep!

    The airplane flies in the sky, in the sky, in the sky.
    The airplane flies in the sky, zoom, zoom, zoom!

    The circus train goes on the tracks, on the tracks, on the tracks.
    The circus train goes on the tracks, choo, choo, choo!
(Continue with truck, bus, etc.)

Materials: Vehicle pictures or objects

TELEPHONE

MATCHING NUMERALS
Each child needs a play telephone. Make number cards with one digit per card. The teacher holds up a series of numerals. The children should find the numerals on the dial and dial them.
Materials: Number cards, play telephone
Variation: Give the students a sheet with a number sequence on it for them to dial.

WHO SHOULD YOU CALL?
Give each child a toy telephone to pretend to call a community helper. Place a variety of community helper pictures and one of the fire fighters in a row. The teacher asks a variety of "if" questions, and the children should yell out the appropriate community helper's name.

> Example: If a house is on fire in your neighborhood, who should you call? (The fireman!)
> If you are sick?
> If you are lost?
> If you want a pizza?
> If your tooth hurts?

Materials: Play phones, pictures of community helpers

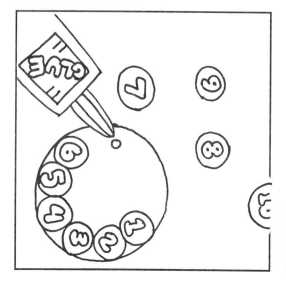

MAKE A DIAL
Supply each child with ten small circles with the numbers zero through nine printed on them. The children should draw and cut out a large circle to represent the telephone dial. Let the children put the numbers in order around the dial and glue them on.
Materials: Paper, glue, scissors
Variation: Print numerals on the dial. The children match the small numerals and then glue them on.

NOT·SO·BORING BASICS

BODY PARTS

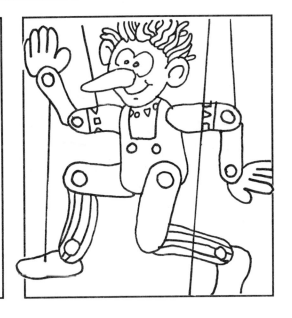

BODY PART SONG
Tune – "I'm A Little Teapot"
I'm a little body, and my head's on top.
My feet can run, they never stop.

My mouth can smile, my hands can clap.
My eyes can see and blink like that!

My arms can bend, my nose can smell.
My fingers can wiggle, my ears as well.
Materials: None

LEGS, LEGS, LEGS
Cut out a variety of legs (fat, short, long, thin, bowed). Let the children select a pair of legs, glue them to paper, and draw the rest of the body.
Materials: Construction paper, glue, crayons, scissors

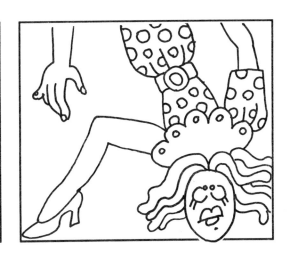

"WHAT'S WRONG?" BODY PART PUZZLES
Cut out a variety of large pictures of people from magazines. Mount these on sturdy paper. Cut apart the different body parts (arms, legs, etc.). The teacher puts the puzzles together incorrectly and the children tell what's wrong with the puzzles.
Materials: Magazine pictures, paper, glue, scissors

NAME THAT BODY PART
Draw a large body on a piece of felt. Attach to a wall or similar surface. Attach/glue strips of removable adhesive to table tennis balls. Let the children throw the balls at the body. Then the children should identify the body part that the ball hits.
Materials: Removable adhesive, felt, table tennis balls

ARMS LENGTH
"Measure" lengths of different body parts using various materials such as, string, pipe cleaners, straws, strips of paper/cloth, etc.
Materials: Materials to be used to measure

MAGIC TOUCH
Make a "magic fairy wand" (a dowel rod with a star at the end). Each child should get a chance to be the "magician." The teacher tells the magician where he/she should touch (ankle, knee, etc.) to have a child perform a certain action. For example: "I touched your knee, now jump."
Materials: Dowel rods, paper star

COLORS

COLOR BLIND

Make a pair of glasses using a plastic frame and colored cellophane. Tell the children that you have a pair of magic glasses or a looking glass that can turn everything in the room a certain color. Tell them that they must say the magic words before looking in the glasses or the looking glass.

Magic Words: Hocus-pocus, abrakazam
      Make everything (name of color) where I am!

Materials: Colored cellophane, plastic glasses frame

Variation: The glasses or looking glass can be shaped like an item which is that color, e.g., red – apple, green – shamrock, orange – pumpkin, yellow – star

Variation II: Make a telescope or binoculars using empty toilet paper or paper towel rolls. Cover each end with cellophane.

COLOR CRAZY

Secretly put drops of food coloring into milk. Watch the children's surprise as they pour a different color milk. You may also enjoy making green mashed potatoes, blue scrambled eggs, etc.

Materials: Food coloring, milk

BURIED COLORS

Bury items of different colors in a plastic swimming pool filled with shredded newspaper, sudsy water, packing styrofoam, or sand. Have each pupil tell the others what color item to find, e.g., find something green.

Materials: Different-colored objects, shredded newspaper, styrofoam pieces, sand, soapy water, large box or plastic tub or pool

COLOR COSTUMES
Let each child paint a grocery sack a different color. Write the color name on the front of the paper sack. Cut out holes for arms and head. Each student should wear a color costume. Child A stands still while others collect items from around the room that match Child A's costume. The teacher may want to use the prompt, "Bring blue things to the blue person," etc.
Materials: Grocery sacks, paint

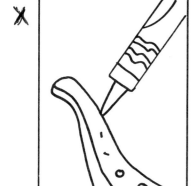

I HAVE NO COLOR
Scatter crayons on the floor. Have outlined pictures of common objects to show to the children. (The pictures should be outlined only, i.e., black and white.) Recite the following song while showing a picture.

> Tune – "Mary Had A Little Lamb"
> My banana has no color, has no color, has no color.
> My banana has no color. What can I do?

A child suggests, points to, or selects the appropriate crayon and then colors the picture. Continue until all the children have a different picture to color.
Materials: Outlined pictures of different objects, crayons

COLOR POTIONS
Tell the children that you want them to help you make some magic "potions." Have them put drops of food coloring in several glasses of clear liquids. Show a picture of a colored animal for each color in a glass (red bird, orange fish, green frog, brown bear, yellow duck, black sheep, blue horse, purple cat). Tell the children to drink a "potion." Then they must act like the corresponding color of the animal. Have the children request the color they want to drink.
Materials: Clear liquids, food coloring, clear glasses, colored pictures of animals

COLOR GARAGES

Collect different-colored match box cars/trucks. Paint small milk cartons the same colors as the cars/trucks. Let the children match the cars/trucks to the same colored garages.

Materials: Toy cars/trucks, paint, small milk cartons

Variation: Place a specific color of car in a garage. Ask the child, "Where is the orange car?" Response: "In the blue garage." Also, vary the locations used, e.g., on top, behind, in front, between, etc.

Variation II: Make roads on the floor or table that the child drives along as he/she takes the car to the same color of garage.

MIX IT UP

Fill clear glasses with water. Make each glass of water a different color by adding food coloring. Have the students find a spoon/stirrer to match the colored water. Let the students sort and put the matching stirrer in water.

Materials: Clear glasses, water, food coloring, colored spoons or drink stirrers

COLOR TOSS

Let the children use scissors to cut different colors of construction paper into small pieces. The teacher gathers the pieces together and drops a handful of paper. Then the children catch whatever pieces they can.

Materials: Scissors, construction paper

LEFT/RIGHT

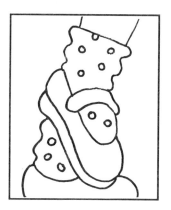

MAKE IT GO
Tune – "Hi Ho, Hi Ho, It's Off To Work We Go!"
Watch me! Watch me!
I'll make my left/right foot/hand move.
I'll shake (wiggle, kick, wave) it fast, I'll shake it slow.
Oh, watch me make my left foot go.
Materials: None

BRACELETS
Make bracelets by cutting pieces of construction paper into strips. Make these strips into a circle and fasten with glue, staples, or tape. Cut out and attach small pictures to the bracelets. Each child should put a bracelet on each wrist. The teacher asks questions regarding where certain pictures are located (on the right bracelet or on the left bracelet).
Materials: Construction paper, pictures, staples, glue, tape

LEFT ONLY – RIGHT ONLY
During a specific activity – for example, a ball game – the children are only allowed to use one hand to play. The children decide before the game which hand everyone must use. As a reminder, have mittens available for the children to wear on the hand they will not use.
Materials: Mittens

QUIET SIDE/NOISY SIDE

Attach bells to elastic loops. Place on the right side of the body (foot, knee, shoulder, wrist, etc.). Use a hairpin to attach the loop to the hair. Give instructions such as, "Move your right hand." The right side should make noise, and the left side should be quiet. Reverse bells at another time.
Materials: Bells

I HAVE TWO HANDS

I have two hands and they're mine.
I like to use them all the time.
There's one on my left and one on my right.
I put my left hand behind me so it's out of sight.
I can raise my right hand high or shake it down low,
I can make my left hand wave fast or wave it real slow.
I have two hands and they're both mine.
I like to use them all the time.
Materials: None

LEFT/RIGHT VESTS

Make paper bag vests. (Cut armholes on sides and large holes in the bottom for the heads.) Instruct the children as to which side is left and which side is right. Cut out various construction paper shapes (stars, circles, trees, cars, etc.). Have the children put on the vests. Let them give directions as to whether to tape their shapes on the left or right side of the vest.
Materials: Paper bag vests, construction paper shapes, scissors, tape

SHAPES

MAKE A STRAW SHAPE

Let the children use straws to make shapes. They can do this activity in imitation of an adult or by following directions from the teacher.
Materials: Straws

SHAPE MARCH

Use large pieces of paper to make shape costumes (like a sandwich sign). Make enough shapes so that each child can wear a costume.
1. Have the shapes march to music.
2. Have shapes follow directions (all circles run to the door).
3. Find a shape that is the same, and dance together.
Materials: Paper, tape, staples, records

A SHAPE IN MY GELATIN

Prepare gelatin. Pour into an ice tray. Put one piece of fruit cocktail in each square. After the gelatin has hardened, let the children identify the shape in the gelatin while they are eating. (You may want to cut a few of the fruit pieces such as peaches, into triangles.)
Materials: Ice cube tray, gelatin, fruit cocktail

SHAPE PEOPLE

Use shapes to make circle, square, or triangle people. (See illustration.) "Shape people" can be pasted on a large sheet of paper cut into that shape also.

Materials: Construction paper shapes of various sizes

SHAPE CATERPILLAR

Give each child a caterpillar's head. (Cut out a large circle, attach antennae, eyes, nose, and mouth.) Give each child a variety of different-colored shapes. As the children name the shape, attach it to the caterpillar.

Materials: Paper, scissors

SHAPE JEWELRY

Make paper jewelry with a variety of shapes. Place the jewelry on a table and attach a price tag to each. (Use amounts of 1 to 10 cents.) Designate a child as a store clerk. Provide the remaining children with ten pennies or play money to buy the shape jewelry. The children should tell the store clerk which piece of shape jewelry they want ("I want the square-shaped necklace."), and then give the clerk the appropriate amount of money. Let the children see themselves in a mirror wearing the shape jewelry.

Materials: Construction paper, glue scissors, table, pennies or play money

SHAPES AND FRIENDS

Scatter different shapes around the classroom on the floor. Use at least three or four of each shape. One child should stand on a shape and say:

> I'm on a shape,
> But I won't say the name.
> ____ , (name) be my friend,
> And find one that's the
> same.

Continue until each child is on one kind of shape, e.g., all the triangles.

Materials: Large paper cutout shapes

SHAPES IN THE HOUSE

> Tune – "Farmer In The Dell"
> Oh, the roof is a triangle,
> And the door is a rectangle
> The clock's a circle, and the
> window's a square.
> There are shapes everywhere.

HOME SHAPES

Tell the children to bring shapes from home: square, triangle, rectangle, circle. Tell them if they bring shapes that are not theirs (such as their mom's square paper weight), to get permission first.

PREPOSITIONS

ACTION SONG
     Tune – "Mary Had A Little Lamb"
     Around the chair, we will march,
     We will march, we will march.
     Around the chair, we will march.
     March around the chair.
Materials: None
Variation: Change the preposition, noun, and/or verb

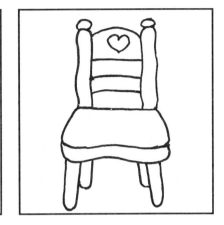

RHYME TIME
Place pictures of a pie, tree, pair of pants, rug, and a girl in front of the children. Say the rhyme, and call upon a child to complete the phrase and place insects on the appropriate picture.
     There's a fly on the _____ (pie).
     There's a bee over the _____ (tree).
     There's an ant in the _____ (pants).
     There's a spider beside _____ (her).
     There's a bug under the _____ (rug).
Materials: Picture(s) of pie; tree; pants; rug; girl; small toy or paper insects – fly, bee, ant, spider, etc.

MOVE THE PAPER PLATE
Give each child a paper plate. Let the children place the paper plates according to the directions given by the teacher or by a fellow classmate. (Example: Put the plate on your head. Put the plate under your leg. Put the plate between your knees, etc.)
Materials: Paper plates

CATCH THE FISH

Cut a goldfish bowl shape out of a center of a 9" x 11" piece of paper. Cover this with a piece of plastic wrap or cellophane. Staple or glue this on three sides to another sheet of construction paper (leaving the top open to insert a fish). Have each child cut out and decorate a goldfish. Make a cat, or use a stuffed cat. Tell the following story:

One day, Sam the cat was very hungry. He was tired of the cat food that his owner always gave him. He decided to eat the family goldfish Harvey. Now, Harvey was very fast and jumped everywhere! When Sam tried to catch him, he jumped on the bowl, in the bowl, under the bowl, in front of the bowl, etc.

As prepositions are stated, the children should place Harvey in the appropriate place.

Materials: Construction paper, cellophane, scissors

Variation: Children place Harvey first telling others where he hid.

WHERE I AM

The teacher directs a child to go in, on, under, beside, between, behind, etc. The rest of the group sings the following song:

Tune – "London Bridge"
John is sitting under the table, under the table, under the table.
John is sitting under the table.
That is where he is.

Materials: None

PUT IT THERE

Cover four or five small milk cartons or juice cans with construction paper. Put one sticker on each container. (The stickers should coordinate with the specific unit being emphasized – animals, fruits, vegetables, shapes, etc.) The teacher directs each child where to put his/her marker. For example, put it under the dog container, behind the sheep container, by the pig container, far away from the duck container, etc.

Materials: Small milk cartons or juice cans, construction paper, stickers, objects to use as markers

FOX FINDS A FRIEND

One day Fox said, "I'm lonely. I think I will go and look for a friend." He ran into a log. He saw a skunk! He ran out of the log. He climbed up a tree. He saw an owl. The owl said, "Whoo-oo." The fox ran down the tree. He dug under a rock. He saw a snake. The snake said, "Ssss-sss." The fox hurried from under the rock. He said, "I will go back to my den." When he got there, he saw two glowing eyes inside. He yelled, "Who's in my house?" "It's just me," said the voice. "I was just looking for a friend." "Me, too," said Fox. "Come out, and we will both be friends."
What do you think came out of the den?
Materials: Felt cutout pieces of the fox, log, tree, skunk, owl, snake, rock, den, eyes; a felt board

WHERE'S THE CEREAL?

At snack time, use pieces of cereal to play a hiding game. Let the children hide a piece of cereal on, under, in back of, in front of, etc., their bowl. Let the other children close their eyes and guess where it is hidden.
Materials: Cereal, bowls

WHERE, OH WHERE

Place objects in various locations around the room (in, on, under, over, beside, etc.). Call upon a child to find a named item as you sing the following song, and allow him/her time to fill in and sing the last line of the song.

   Where, oh where is the _____ (item name) ?
   Oh _____ (child's name), find it for me!

Materials: Various classroom objects or toys

LETTERS & NUMBERS

HOMES FOR THE LETTERS/NUMBERS

Draw several simple houses on separate sheets of paper. Write a letter in each doorway. Cut out paper doors equivalent in size to the drawn doors. Write corresponding letters on the cutout doors. Let the children match the doors to the houses using the letters to discriminate placement of each door.

Materials: Paper, markers, scissors
Variation: Substitute numerals

MESSY ALPHABET/NUMERALS

Have the children form letters on a vertical or horizontal surface while verbalizing what they made. Use plastic squirt guns, spray bottles, shaving cream, whipped cream in a can, etc., to make the letters.

Materials: Squirt gun, spray bottle, shaving cream, whipped cream in a can, large piece of paper
Variation: Children tell each other what letter to make.
Variation II: Substitute numerals.

TOUCHABLE ALPHABET/NUMERALS

Cut out the letters of the alphabet from foam rubber carpet padding. Have the children:

    Make prints using water or finger paint.
    Put them in a bag and have the children
        identify by feeling the shape.
    Throw several around the room and run to get
        the one requested by someone else.
    Follow directions with a letter, e.g., if you have
        an "A," put it on your foot.
    Sequence three or four letters as instructed.

Materials: Foam rubber carpet padding, finger paint, bag
Variation: Substitute numerals

ALPHABET/NUMERAL CAKEWALK

Place approximately ten different letters of the alphabet in a circle on the floor. The teacher or student picks one of the letters to be the "star" letter, e.g., "M." As the music is played, the pupils walk around the letters. When the music stops, the pupils stop on the nearest letter. The child who stops on the star letter yells, "I stopped on the M. I'm a star!"

Materials: Record player, ten letters or numbers

Variation: The children walk around the letters. When the music stops, the caller calls out a letter. The child standing on the letter called identifies himself/herself.

Variation II: Substitute numerals.

EYE DOCTOR

Print a row of 5 inch letters on a large chart, and then print rows of 4 inch, 3 inch, and 2 inch letters. Place a chair approximately 3 feet from the chart. One child is chosen to be the eye doctor and puts on a white jacket and is given a pointer stick. The children take turns visiting the eye doctor who asks them to name the letters that he/she points to.

Materials: Chart paper, marker, chair, white jacket or large white shirt, pointer

Variation: Substitute numerals

ALPHABET/NUMERAL BEADS

Use a marker to write letters on a variety of wooden stringing beads. Then give each child several beads to string. Ask each child to name beads as he/she strings them.

Materials: Wooden beads, marker, string

Variation: Substitute numerals.

Variation II: Have a child find all the beads with a specified letter.

ALPHABET/NUMBER COOKIES

Make a cookie monster from a tall box (cover the entire box with blue paper, cut out a large mouth, and include appropriate features). Cut tagboard cookies small enough to fit into his/her mouth. Write a letter on each of the cookies. Pretend that the cookie monster wants to eat a specific letter cookie, e.g., an "H" cookie. The child should find the correct cookie and feed the cookie monster.
Materials: Cardboard box, colored paper, tagboard
Variation: Substitute numerals.

MOTOR ALPHABET/NUMERALS

Place the letters of the alphabet at one end of the room. Use a motor activity to get the requested letter (ride a skateboard, roll or crawl, pull a friend in a wagon, push a toy shopping cart, etc.).
Materials: Cutout letters, skateboard, wagon, cart, etc.
Variation: Substitute numerals.

ALPHABET/NUMERAL SOUP

Hide plastic/magnetic letters in a tub of beans, packing styrofoam, shredded paper, etc. Let the children search through the material and pull out a letter. The child should name that letter and give a word that begins with that letter, e.g., "B" for "baby." If applicable, the children can put the letters in order on a magnetic board as they pull out more letters.
Materials: Plastic magnetic letters; shredded paper, beans, packing styrofoam, etc.; medium-sized tub; magnetic board
Variation: Substitute numerals.

116

SKILLS CHARTS

Nature's Nuances	Absurdities, Creativity, Imagination	Art	Associations/ Comparisons	Fine Motor	Following Directions	Gross Motor	Interpersonal Relationships	Math	Music, Rhythm, Rhyme	Problem-Solving	Science	Sensory Integration	Sequencing
1. Ants		✓	✓	✓	✓	✓	✓	✓	✓		✓	✓	✓
2. Bees		✓	✓	✓	✓	✓	✓	✓	✓		✓	✓	✓
3. Butterfly/Caterpillars		✓	✓		✓	✓		✓	✓		✓		✓
4. Eggs	✓	✓	✓	✓	✓		✓	✓	✓		✓		✓
5. Fish/Ocean	✓	✓	✓	✓	✓	✓		✓	✓		✓	✓	
6. Moon and Stars	✓	✓	✓	✓	✓	✓		✓			✓		✓
7. Owls	✓	✓	✓	✓	✓	✓		✓	✓		✓		✓
8. Rain	✓		✓	✓	✓	✓		✓	✓	✓	✓		✓
9. Seeds and Plants	✓	✓	✓	✓	✓			✓	✓	✓			✓
10. Snow	✓	✓		✓	✓			✓	✓			✓	✓
11. Squirrels	✓	✓	✓	✓	✓			✓	✓		✓	✓	✓
12. Sun and Clouds	✓	✓	✓	✓	✓		✓	✓	✓		✓	✓	
13. Wind	✓		✓		✓				✓	✓	✓	✓	
14. Worms	✓	✓	✓	✓	✓	✓		✓			✓	✓	✓

There is a skill chart for each section. Each subsection is listed in alphabetical order for easy reference, and the activities within the subsection encourage use/development of the checked skills.

This time-saver not only allows you to see at a glance what skills a particular subsection emphasizes, but it also speeds your activity planning when you want to focus on a particular skill. Also included is a blank chart for you to fill in your own activities!

Nature's Nuances

	Sequencing	Sensory Integration	Science	Problem-Solving	Music, Rhythm, Rhyme	Math	Interpersonal Relationships	Gross Motor	Following Directions	Fine Motor	Associations/ Comparisons	Art	Absurdities, Creativity, Imagination
1. Ants	✓	✓	✓		✓	✓	✓	✓	✓	✓	✓	✓	
2. Bees	✓	✓	✓		✓	✓	✓	✓	✓	✓	✓	✓	
3. Butterfly/Caterpillars	✓		✓		✓	✓		✓	✓		✓	✓	
4. Eggs	✓	✓	✓		✓	✓	✓		✓	✓	✓	✓	✓
5. Fish/Ocean			✓		✓	✓		✓	✓	✓	✓	✓	✓
6. Moon and Stars	✓		✓			✓		✓	✓	✓	✓	✓	✓
7. Owls	✓		✓		✓	✓		✓	✓	✓	✓	✓	✓
8. Rain	✓			✓	✓	✓		✓	✓	✓	✓	✓	✓
9. Seeds and Plants	✓			✓	✓	✓			✓	✓	✓	✓	✓
10. Snow	✓	✓			✓	✓	✓		✓	✓		✓	✓
11. Squirrels	✓	✓	✓		✓	✓			✓	✓	✓	✓	✓
12. Sun and Clouds		✓	✓	✓	✓	✓			✓	✓	✓		✓
13. Wind		✓	✓		✓				✓		✓	✓	✓
14. Worms	✓	✓	✓	✓		✓		✓	✓	✓		✓	✓

119

Getting To Know You

	Sequencing	Sensory Integration	Science	Problem-Solving	Music, Rhythm, Rhyme	Math	Interpersonal Relationships	Gross Motor	Following Directions	Fine Motor	Associations/ Comparisons	Art	Absurdities, Creativity, Imagination
1. Chef	✓	✓		✓		✓		✓	✓	✓	✓	✓	
2. Friends					✓		✓	✓	✓		✓	✓	
3. Homemaker				✓	✓		✓	✓	✓	✓	✓	✓	
4. Mail Carrier				✓	✓		✓	✓	✓	✓	✓		
5. Teacher				✓	✓		✓		✓	✓	✓		✓

Going Places	Sequencing	Sensory Integration	Science	Problem-Solving	Music, Rhythm, Rhyme	Math	Interpersonal Relationships	Gross Motor	Following Directions	Fine Motor	Associations/Comparisions	Art	Absurdities, Creativity, Imagination
1. Circus	✓				✓	✓	✓	✓	✓	✓	✓	✓	✓
2. Groceries	✓				✓			✓	✓		✓	✓	✓
3. Ice Cream	✓				✓	✓	✓	✓	✓	✓	✓	✓	✓
4. Library	✓			✓		✓	✓		✓	✓	✓	✓	
5. Restaurant	✓			✓	✓		✓	✓	✓	✓		✓	

Dress 'Em Up

	Absurdities, Creativity, Imagination	Art	Associations/ Comparisons	Fine Motor	Following Directions	Gross Motor	Interpersonal Relationships	Math	Music, Rhythm, Rhyme	Problem-Solving	Science	Sensory Integration	Sequencing
1. Clothes	✓	✓	✓		✓			✓	✓	✓			
2. Fasteners	✓	✓	✓	✓	✓		✓		✓	✓			✓
3. Hats	✓		✓		✓	✓	✓	✓	✓				
4. Shoes/Socks/Feet	✓	✓	✓	✓	✓	✓		✓	✓	✓		✓	✓
5. Winter Wear	✓		✓	✓	✓		✓	✓	✓	✓		✓	

Holiday Spirits

Holiday Spirits	Sequencing	Sensory Integration	Science	Problem-Solving	Music, Rhythm, Rhyme	Math	Interpersonal Relationships	Gross Motor	Following Directions	Fine Motor	Associations/ Comparisons	Art	Absurdities, Creativity, Imagination
1. Bells				✓	✓		✓	✓	✓		✓		✓
2. Elves	✓			✓	✓				✓		✓		✓
3. Ornaments	✓			✓	✓	✓	✓		✓	✓	✓	✓	✓
4. Pilgrims & Indians	✓			✓	✓	✓	✓	✓	✓	✓	✓	✓	✓
5. Reindeer	✓			✓	✓	✓	✓	✓	✓	✓	✓	✓	✓
6. Scarecrows	✓				✓	✓	✓	✓	✓	✓	✓	✓	✓
7. Turkeys						✓			✓	✓	✓	✓	✓
8. Wreaths		✓				✓	✓	✓	✓	✓		✓	✓

Useful Items	Furniture	Object Functions	Telephone	Tools	Vehicles
Sequencing		✓	✓	✓	
Sensory Integration				✓	
Science					
Problem-Solving	✓	✓	✓	✓	✓
Music, Rhythm, Rhyme		✓	✓	✓	✓
Math			✓	✓	
Interpersonal Relationships	✓		✓		✓
Gross Motor					
Following Directions	✓	✓	✓	✓	✓
Fine Motor	✓		✓	✓	✓
Associations/Comparisions	✓	✓	✓	✓	✓
Art	✓		✓	✓	
Absurdities, Creativity, Imagination	✓	✓	✓	✓	✓

1. Furniture
2. Object Functions
3. Telephone
4. Tools
5. Vehicles

Not-So-Boring Basics

	Sequencing	Sensory Integration	Science	Problem-Solving	Music, Rhythm, Rhyme	Math	Interpersonal Relationships	Gross Motor	Following Directions	Fine Motor	Associations/ Comparisons	Art	Absurdities, Creativity, Imagination
1. Body Parts				✓	✓	✓	✓	✓	✓	✓	✓		✓
2. Colors	✓	✓	✓					✓	✓	✓	✓	✓	✓
3. Left/Right				✓	✓			✓	✓	✓			
4. Letters & Numbers	✓	✓			✓	✓		✓	✓	✓		✓	✓
5. Shapes		✓			✓			✓	✓		✓	✓	
6. Prepositions				✓	✓			✓	✓	✓	✓	✓	✓

	1.	2.	3.	4.	5.	6.	7.	8.	9.	10.	11.	12.	13.	14.	15.

NOTES